AN
ALEMBIC
OF
PHILOSOPHY

PAUL O'HERRON

For Mary Rose and John,
my mother and father

Thanks to all who helped, who endured,
who lit the way, who left prints, who missed things
displaced by the effort to make the book:

Rebecca, my wife. My children: Stephen, Teresa,
Siobhan, Audrey, Petra, Micaela, Ruth and Thomas.

My sisters and brothers: Jeanne, John, Tom, Ray and Jim.

Stephen John Carroll, Mary Clark, Dan Marcellus,
Mary Whelan.

Philosophers from Parmenides to Pieper and Prufer.

My students and teachers.

Myriad others—many of you are hidden from me.

"...the achieve of, the mastery of the thing..."
– Gerard Manley Hopkins
Windhover

"In philosophical argument, he who loses,
gains the most because he learns the most."
– Epicurus
Vatican Sayings, LXXIV

Contents

Introduction

This work introduces philosophy by distilling six themes and some fundamental distinctions or 'tools' in its alembic.
Philosophy asks three things: wonder, insight and distinctions. Wonder is the ! and the ? and again the !. Wonder is a wonderful thing. It moves from one thing to another. A child wonders how the world can be round, how numbers can go on forever. A scientist would wonder if things were otherwise. Can we do anything about wonder? Maybe. Sadly some people close up and lose the wonder we all began with. Philosophy is for the young at mind!
Insight is just what it says. Seeing into things. Can anyone take a crash course in insight? As seeing depends on looking, so insight depends on taking thought, on wonder. If we think about things and "stay in the truth", the right thoughts may come. Bach said that in writing his music he felt he was "taking dictation".
Insight is a close relative of intuition. Intuition gives us a grasp of 'first principles' -the things you start with to make an argument or joined reasoning. Without it philosophy never connects to reality. It becomes a verbal game, a gallery or museum of flashy but floating concepts.
And philosophy is often taught this way - as a parade of schools and isms, of possible and historical stances on a host of positions. High flying, but restless and nestless.
This is tedious, boring and rootless. The learner is left with the idea that if these great intellects can't agree, how can he/she possibly decide.
This book takes the opposite view. Philosophy really is about something. It can land with its feet on the ground. And it has al-

ready gone deeply into the truth of a few things. We are all yoked to wonder. We are all 'in the middle' -neither godlike above wonder nor thinglike beneath. What can be done to make us better philosophers? Two helps: we can learn from others and we can pay careful attention to distinctions.

Descartes and Husserl on consciousness, Hegel on dialectic, Kant on morality, Heidegger and Augustine on time, Thomas on existence, Newton on motion, Plato on beauty, Aristotle on logic - are gems strewn along the paths of thought. Let us turn these over carefully in the light.

Distinctions are the tools of philosophy. They can [almost] be carried around in a box. They can be used in an emergency. Although philosophers do not all share the same distinctions, once a good distinction has been made it tends to stick. If distinctions are blurred, thought is lost. Mortimer Adler says that John Locke and others mistook ideas for"that which we know" instead of "that by which we know". He says this cost philosophy 300 years of fruitless struggle.

Part II discusses several key distinctions, although we also develop some as we discuss the themes.

What is philosophy, anyway? The word means 'love of wisdom'. Not sophology–the science of wisdom. Nobody guarantees we get wisdom. Our questions outrun our answers.

A provisional definition might be that philosophy is the use of (human) reason on almost everything, but especially on the big questions: What is? How to be happy? When an area of inquiry gets very specific and narrowed, philosophy can spin it off to a speciality department. 2500 years ago the celestial bodies were big mysteries. Today they are not as mysterious. The question 'why are the stars up there?' might be philosophical, but the questions 'how far is the sun?' or 'what is the moon made of?' are now subject to very specific inquiry. So these can be separated from the big questions and spun off to the astronomy department.

We compare philosophy to natural science in another way: A scientist may study in great detail the chemical reactions involved in a leaf's changing color; the philosopher may ask "what does a tree experience, what is it like to be a tree?".

Scientists experiment to test and strain reality. Their abstruse and complex mathematics helps reason about the result. But usually the framework itself is given. Chemistry assumes the existence and change of substances. Philosophy asks both about other things and about itself. The question 'what is chemistry' is not a chemical question. The question 'what is philosophy' is a philosophical one. This makes philosophy look foolish, tripping over itself, stumbling on the ? and the ! even when the subject seems so simple. 'What is a thing?', 'What are people for?' 'What is the meaning of meaning?', 'Why do we ask why?' - on an ordinary day these thoughts seem foolish or babyish or vacant.

Yet if no one reflected on such, the human noetic [intellectual] theater would feature only episodes, brilliantly staged perhaps, but unconnected to any play. Is philosophy useful? Something is useful if it serves some other purpose. Philosophy is for itself. But like pure mathematics, it can confer benefits elsewhere -politics, education, etc.–even if only by dispelling false views.

If it is done for itself, philosophy must be fun. Its off-beat questions (what does God do?, what is 'now'?) and its unusual words show this playfulness.

If, like me, you spend a fair time thinking on things that simply don't exist, *"meonic"* (of non-being) should be in your verbal quiver. Would you like to speak to Hegel? Just use a prosopopoeia. *Quodlibetal* (what[ever] pleases) is a word we have from medieval disputations where questions were asked freely. It has all five vowels in reverse order and may be used quodlibetally.

Philosophy is as universal, big, and free as intellect itself. Strictly, there are no schools or national types of philosophy. It can't be pre-cast or told what to think about. If truth is a constraint, philosophy is constrained. We may be brought beyond human reason, but we cannot hold it back.

How far does philosophy reach? Is it the highest human activity? For Aristotle, it is. Philosophizing is the highest joy and "something divine" in us. For Aquinas, it comes in second. After ten million words: *"Non possum, quia omnia quae scripsi, videntur mihi paleae."* [I cannot (finish the book) because all I have written seems like straw to me.]

Surprisingly perhaps, originality is not important. Thoughts original to you may have been thought by the cave painters at Lascaux–so what? The truth is what counts.

While the scholarship here is accurate, even the best scholars can't trace each idea back to its first expression. We don't try to. Nor do we crowd each statement with every possible qualifier–this would choke off interest. But philosophy is concerned with its own history and we include many historical positions here.

This is "an alembic" not "the alembic"–while it aims to cover much of what is central to philosophy, other selections and emphases are possible. To the extent the work has a deliberate bias, it favors those who think philosophy is possible. Sceptics, and those bogged down in a problem like "How can we know at all", are left alone. If you take swimming lessons you don't spend time on whether swimming is possible.

Some parts are more complex or deeper than others. This pulls some readers forward, while giving each type of learner something. It also encourages reading the sources in full. To the extent the book can stand on its own, it 'stands on the shoulders of giants'. Thank you, giants! I take credit for the shortcomings. They get the 'longcomings'.

The book can be a college text (to go with a teacher whom it may complement), or be a door for the autodidact (self-tutor) or the opsimath (late learner). May it set off a few intellectual jousts! It's for the reluctant and for every type of beginner. For the fun of it!

So we can jump in quickly, footnotes, references, and questions are put at the end of each chapter. A recommended reading list is at the end.

HAPPINESS

I. Introduction

II. What is it?
  A. Finite
    i. Positive Notions
      Aristotle
      Epicurus
      Kant

    ii. Negative Notions
      Sophocles
      Marx
      Hobbes
      Epictetus

    iii. Can it be reached?
      Aristotle
      Mill
  B. Infinite
      Nietzsche
      Sankara
      Buddhism
      Western Theology
      Pieper

III. A Coda

IV. Footnotes and References

V. Questions

I. Introduction

What is happiness? Our interest is not just an abstract one. We can sit back and ponder 'what is time?', but we actually want to be happy, not just look at it from afar. Is happiness one thing or many? Is it something we have (a possession) or do (an activity) or are (a condition)? Is it a process or a goal or neither? Is it the same for different types of people? Is it easy or hard? common or rare? Is it in our power or does it come from without (other people, fate, luck, God)? To be happy must you know you are happy? If you think you are happy, are you? Is happiness open to everyone? Can we stay happy? Are there degrees of happiness? Do we have to change to fit the higher kinds of joy? Many lines of inquiry.

One question we should face right away: Is happiness a subjective thing–basically whatever you think it is or elect that it should be, or is it an objective thing–pretty much the same for everybody regardless of one's opinions?

The subjective notion involves the kind of evaluations involved in selecting a menu or a wardrobe. The objective idea may be illustrated by an example from nutrition. Suppose I prefer cadmium to carbohydrates and riches to loyalty. Carbohydrates supply the body with needed energy; cadmium is poisonous. I can prefer whatever I do prefer, but I cannot make cadmium good for me. The objective theory says that some preferences bring unhappiness no matter what, while others, because they are lined up with my 'real nature', tend to bring happiness (unless something else supervenes).

In modern secular societies, the subjective theory is often assumed. Thomas Jefferson wrote of the inalienable right to "Life, Liberty and the pursuit of Happiness."[1] Does he mean life and liberty are definite things but happiness is whatever you wish to pursue (as long as you don't interfere with someone else's pursuit)?

What about an empirical study of happiness? We conduct surveys on how happy people are and on what makes them happy.

Statistics are gathered relating happiness to other variables. Are people happier in warmer climates? What is the effect of foods, times of the day, types of work, music, colors? Such a social science approach would run into severe limits. If a criminal gloats over his crime and a hero is hesitant or depressed will we accept these indications at face value? Also, such a science would be silent about happiness beyond earthly life.

But, in fact, such a science has hardly been thought of. Even the Encyclopedia of Philosophy [2] scarcely looks at happiness. It has a scant two pages on it, but gives over a hundred pages to logic. Is this due to the widespread but largely unexamined notion that happiness is whatever you think it is, and so not subject to a valid science? Yet isn't it odd that an age which so glories in its science, casts no light on happiness?

If we buy a purely subjective theory of happiness, it dissolves as a theme for philosophy. But before we decide let us look closely at some arguments that claim happiness is a fairly definite thing. We hone our intellects on their extraordinary thought about ordinary things, while we ponder where the truth lies.

To simplify things, let us use a prosopopoeia (a figure of speech in which the absent or dead are present and speak directly to us).

II. What is it?

A. Finite
i. Positive Notions

ARISTOTLE
Actions are for something (even if for the fun of it). A means is something which is for something else (building is for shelter); an end is the purpose or goal (the finished house which provides shelter).

A subtle distinction is brought up right away. Some activities aim at an external product such as building a house. This kind of activity is a process or *dynamis*. But there are activities whose fullness and purpose rather ride along with the action itself, such as dancing, conversing with friends, playing, and perhaps, living itself. This kind of activity is an actuality or *energeia*. Not everything is a process or is for a product.

Means can be hooked up like railroad cars:

Equip a horse> Ride better> Fight better> Win battle> Win war
A ———> B———> C———> D———> E

Here A is a means for B. B, C and D are both means and ends. E is the final goal (of this series). Lacking a final goal, intermediates lose orientation. An apparently rational set of acts is washed out in absurdity. If Joseph Stalin deliberately let the Communists lose the Spanish Civil War, what difference would it make to him whether the horses were well equipped? It is common to lose sight of goals in our absorption with means, but it's headsplitting chaos to have means that are not aimed at anything at all.

The 'final end' or 'ultimate goal' is that purpose toward which all other purposes aim. Such is desired for itself alone and not as a means to something else. It is 'final' logically, not temporally -not because it comes at the end of life but because it terminates any series of means.

(Most) everyone agrees that happiness is the final end. We do x, y, z to be happy. But we don't seek to be happy so we can do x, y, or z. As life goes on, we don't constantly think of our ultimate end. But if there is one, "will not the knowledge of it, then, have a great influence on life? Shall we not, like archers who have a mark to aim at, be more likely to hit upon what is right?" (1094a23-25)[3]

So happiness is the final end -but what fills the bill? It may clear things up to consider what it is not. Many people say it is wealth, health, honor (we might add glory or power) or pleasure.

Wealth: Wealth (or, at least, money) can't be right because it is a means. But we are looking for the end. Money is for what can be bought with it. We notice this if it suddenly loses value as a medium of exchange (Confederate money after the Civil War). What we really want are the goodies money can get for us. Only a miser directly loves money as an object in itself (he fills the tub with money and climbs in). The miser is probably beyond help, but quite rare. Everyone else can be cured by Dr. Aristotle's philosophicotherapy.

Health: Health is chiefly a means. We notice it when we don't have it. Once we feel good again, we look around for something to do. A blind man cured is ecstatic, but then he wants to get on with seeing things.

Honor: Honor is in the one honoring, not in the one honored. Jesus was hailed on Palm Sunday but crucified on Good Friday. The change in attitude and hence the attitude itself occurs in those honoring. Further, one could be honored without even knowing it, or for something undeserved (honoring the wrong person for an invention), or by those whose adulation has little basis. (Einstein's name became synonymous for genius among many who had no idea what he said.) So honor is a frail thing to hang happiness on.

[Power seems either a means (you can get things with it) or it is a matter of the honor and glory that come with it.]

Pleasure: Pleasure is tentatively accepted as a good in itself and/or as a rider that goes along with other goods. But by pleasure the 'man in the street' means physical gratification. This is too low a goal for humans because it engages only part of our being.

So we ask once more–what is happiness? Granted we are looking for a final end, but do humans have a final end? It seems man is for something because the parts and arts of man have purpose. Eye and ear have definite functions relating to the whole man. Wouldn't it be odd if the parts have purpose, but the whole person had no purpose! Can the carburetor and tires have purpose but the car itself have none?

Shipbuilding, medicine, plumbing–each have their own techniques which aim at definite goals (navigation, health, sanitation). Again, if man as doctor has a purpose, and man as plumber has a purpose–wouldn't it be strange if man as man had no purpose! if the overall activity of being human had no rhyme or reason!

But if we have a purpose, how can we find it? To find the purpose of a thing take a look at it, focus on what is special about it. A hammer has a handle, but so does a baseball bat. The purpose of a hammer is more indicated by its metal part. A shoe can be used to carry grapes but that doesn't explain why it is not in grape shape.

What's distinctive about humans? Thinking, and speaking together about what is and what is to be done–rationality, *logos*.

As a hammer is for hammering, a violin for "violining", so a human is for "humaning". Further, the violining of violinist and violin lies most in the actual playing, not merely in being potential, not just as skill and instrument. If violinist and ballplayer never actually play, then it is only in a very shrivelled sense that they are violinist or ballplayer.

So for humans to really be, to do the "human thing", they must be rational, and actively so. A third note is needed. When we say we want something done, normally we automatically mean that it be done fairly well. "Call a plumber!" means call a plumber who can fix the leak; "add these figures" means add them correctly. So our rational activity is to be done well.

Thus the prescription: happiness is excellent rational activity or "virtue" (*arete*).

This is the core of human happiness. Arete is well translated as "excellence". It carries the brave feeling of big hearted nobleness, not righteous narrowness. The menu of happiness has many other items, some even necessary, but these relish and enhance the main dish. We do need health, leisure, even luck, and especially friends.

Let us hold off judging his theory and instead clear away some misconceptions. Many people reject any notion of human purpose. For some the question "what are people for" is unintelligible or childish. For others life is too full of suffering and sadness to think it purposeful. Sartre rejects the idea of human nature to protect human freedom[4].

Aristotle is not so much making special claims (about God, freedom or evil) as simply asking us to look at humans as we look at violins to see what they are all about.

Is he really just saying "do your job well"? No! That puts practical workaday concerns in the forefront. But for Aristotle contemplation is supreme. Rationality is either for itself (contemplation) or governs something else. The latter involves ethics, politics, technology, economics, etc. Six reasons for the supremacy of contemplation are:

1) It is the best activity since both "of the best thing in us" (mind) and of the highest eternal truths.

2) It is the most continuous kind of activity we can do.

3) It is either the most pleasant activity or at least a very pure pleasure unalloyed with pain, guilt, or need.

4) It is most self-sufficient. Justice and bravery lean on others to be just to and brave for. But contemplation can be done alone

or with others, without special equipment, etc.

5,6) It is most an end or goal and it is most leisurely. Practical activity (building, war, statesmanship) is for some other goal. War is not waged in order that there be war; politics is to provide well being, peace and, hence, in the last analysis,leisure.

EPICURUS

History misunderstands Epicurus. His name has come to mean nearly the opposite of what he stood for.

Happiness lies in the understanding of nature and human ways; thankfulness for existence; freedom from false opinions and superstitions; escape from the vanities, turmoils and harangues of public life; virtuous action; and above all in the comity and conversation of friends.

Especially do not fear death: "...death is of no concern to us since all good and evil lie in sensation and sensation ends with death. Therefore, the true belief that death is nothing to us makes a mortal life happy, not by adding to it an infinite time, but by taking away the desire for immortality. So, he too is foolish who says that he fears death, not because it will be painful when it comes, but because the anticipation of it is painful; for that which is no burden when it is present gives pain to no purpose when it is anticipated. Death, the most dreaded of evils, is therefore of no concern to us; for while we exist death is not present, and when death is present we no longer exist. It is therefore nothing either to the living or to the dead since it is not present to the living, and the dead no longer are." (Letter to Menoeceus, p.54)[5]

We and all things exist by the joining of atoms. The blessed gods (who dwell between the worlds) are immortal because their atoms are replenished continuously. But they do not know human affairs, so there is no providence. Yet since nature does well to man, she is beneficent though not benevolent. By using his enlightened free will to stay close to beneficient nature, man assimilates himself as far as possible to the happy gods.

Today we hear this philosophy like a song from a faraway land. Its tone and tune elude us. Our own times are crowded with stirring and striving for progress, self-improvement, the domination of others or nature. And despite his irenic words, death as annihilation and the absence of divine love aren't cozy ideas to many of us.

Yet epicurean man is mild, joyful and intelligent. For him happiness is easy, nearby and deep–but not the deep of sleep, nor the impassivity of being beyond hurt. He is no Stoic grimly self-reliant in the face of encircling evil. Two more quotes to catch his lyricism: "Friendship dances through the world bidding us all to awaken to the recognition of happiness." and "In a philosophical dispute, he gains most who is defeated, since he learns most."(Vatican Sayings, lii and lxxiv)

KANT

Kant does not put his money on happiness but he has something very important to say about deserving it. He says:[6]

1) A 'good will' is the only pure and unalloyed good.

2) One acting out of a good will, acts out of duty, for what should be done, not for his own happiness.

3) Duty points to the Categorical Imperative: Act so your action could be made into a general maxim, a law for all.

4)Happiness is not brought about by thinking (which even increases the dissatisfaction of the sensitive), nor does nature provide it.

5) Acting out of duty makes one "worthy to be happy", not happy. If there is God and immortality presumably the worthy will be made happy. [See Existence of God and Immortality]

What about Kant's idea of happiness? He seems to view it as satisfaction, an equation between desire and fulfillment. If this is all happiness is, then the bright and sensitive have a hard time being happy, since they desire much and are hurt easily. But what of someone who wants very little, or even of one who fulfills base desires? Are we to say the crass and the criminal are truly happy? Of course, no one wants to be frustrated. But isn't satisfaction a property of happiness rather than its essence? [White is a property of snow not its essence.]

ii. Negative Notions

If you think there is some best thing, you probably think attaining it is happiness. But some think in terms of some worst thing.

Avoiding or overcoming this evil is happiness or the closest we can get to it. The best is called the *summum bonum*, the supreme good; the worst is the *summum malum*, the supreme bad. Here we group a few who view happiness so darkly.

Sartre says our existence is anxious and nauseous. Man is outside himself, condemned to want to be what he can never be (God). For him there is no exit.

SOPHOCLES
For Sophocles there is an exit, but better is no entrance. Who could put it more starkly?[7]

me phunai ton ha panta nika logon. to d', epei phane, binai keis hopothen per hekei polu deuteron hos taxista.

Never to have been born is past all prizing, best; but once a man has seen the light, the next best by far, is that he should with all speed to whence he came.

MARX
Two great evils are exploitation and alienation. A worker is exploited when the value of what he produces is greater than what he is paid. If an owner sells a product of someone else's labor we write the equation:

Profit = Price − Cost of Labor = Value Produced − Wages Paid

If an owner charges $120 for an item that he paid his workers $50 to produce, the $70 is profit. The greater the profit or the lower the wages paid, the greater the exploitation. (Note that all costs, even raw materials, are considered labor costs because no one but humans are paid. No one pays the earth for the copper it yields.) Only when unearned profit is eliminated do workers receive the full fruits of their labor.[8]

Alienation occurs when one person's being is turned over to another. The worker or peasant loses himself to his labor and his labor to the owner. Estranged from himself, he begins to view himself as a tool of his own tools. He works all night because "it doesn't make sense" to let expensive machines sit idle. Alienation becomes more extreme the farther the work is from free human interests, the more machine-like, the less thoughtful, the lower the pay, the longer the hours, etc. The marxian vision is to be achieved by changing the forces and structures of society through the socialist and then communist revolutions. How do these thoughts make a theory of happiness? Perhaps the space for happiness will open up when these evils are no more. Unalienated, unexploited man will be curious and alert to the world about him, will fall in love, read good literature, appreciate the arts, sow and reap according to the maxim "to each according to his needs, from each according to his means". This is sketchy. Little is said directly about the good life.

Criticism of Marx has been that his ideas are "good in theory" but "they don't work". We raise a theoretical question: Is marxian happiness enough? Or is it, at best, a comfortable cocoon, far below our existential yearnings?

HOBBES

Reality is material; as centers of little motions in and out (desires and endeavors) we are necessarily self-centered; each person wants more and more. Pleonexia is the desire for more and more. This leads to the war of all against all. But death takes away everything and death in chaotic violence takes away honor as well as life. Life under these 'natural' conditions is "solitary, poor, nasty, brutish, and short". To overcome these evils, we agree not to kill or harm each other by turning our rights over to the sovereign power. We contract out of the 'jungle' and into civil society. Morality is to obey the law. The pressure to do so is not conscience but the awareness of what life without society would be. [9]

Happiness, then, is life in civil society to be enjoyed as much as the laws and one's own situation permit.

Observing human behavior e.g., "behind the wheel", one may say Hobbes' vision of human nature isn't all wrong! But he missed an important distinction. He failed to note that there are 'goodies' of which it is possible to have more and more without cutting down on anyone else's share. Learning or love. Thomas Prufer explains that if he comes to class with a cheese sandwich and a keen understanding of the Pythagorean Theorem, he can share his understanding (but not the sandwich) without losing any of it himself. In fact, his understanding of it may be increased in being shared. This changes a key point in the relation between happiness and pleonexia. If we concentrate on goodies that are noncompetitive, pleonexia does not lead to conflict and so we do not need totalitarian politics to control ourselves.

EPICTETUS

The world divides into things under our control and things not under our control. Many physical things are usually under our control, e.g. what we eat. But externals generally are not under our control. We may be in jail and not free to choose our menus. But we can control our desires and thoughts. For example, even if we might harm someone accidentally, we certainly can control wishing to harm him.

The secret of happiness is to put your eggs in the basket under your control, to have the right will and attitude. Unhappiness comes from desiring what is not under your control and then being frustrated when you don't get it. As for the parts we cannot control, take comfort in God. We are actors in a play and "if it be His pleasure that you play a poor man—act it well". [10]

These ideas may help us face deep tribulation. His is a theistic stoicism flecked with gems–diamonds tough against being bruised by life. But is he saying this?: The good or excellence of a thing is something intrinsic to it (so e.g., if you are free to choose your food, please do choose what is truly nutritious) and not intrinsic to it (so that if you don't get something, don't be upset, you aren't really missing anything because only your desiring made it a good).

Epictetus fits his own philosophy dramatically. He was a slave. But it is a fallacy to confuse (psychoanalyzing) the man with (analyzing) his ideas [*ad hominem* fallacy] or to confuse the origin of a thing with its essence. Van Gogh's paintings are not poor or desperate because he may have been. Having said that, we still thrill to see that in the small room of great thinkers of the ages there stands a slave!

iii. Can it be reached?

ARISTOTLE

After coming down so solidly for contemplation, he immediately wonders: "But such a life would be too high for man; for it is not in so far as he is man that he will live so, but in so far as something divine is present in him;... But we must not follow those who advise us, being men, to think of human things, and being mortal, of mortal things, but must, so far as we can, make ourselves immortal, and strain every nerve to live in accordance with the best thing in us; for even if it be small in bulk much more does it in power and worth surpass everything." [11]

Only a few can reach the high happiness and these but fleetingly. Strictly this is not an argument against any 'definition' or essence of happiness. Whatever something is, that it is, whether we can attain it or not. Some anthropologists say the Aztecs had a serious problem getting enough protein. But they don't deny protein is required for life.

Yet if happiness were totally unattainable, why think on it? But is it so hard and rare?

MILL

Yes!, happiness is possible for an ordinary person in an ordinary life. In his *Utilitarianism* [12] , Mill develops an ethics based on the principle: act for the greatest good of the greatest number. This good is happiness which is pleasure which is mostly mental pleasure. Mental pleasures are those that are alloyed to noble feelings, intellectual tastes and high aspirations. They are far superior to bodily pleasure because:

1) "... those who are equally acquainted with, and equally capable of appreciating and enjoying, both, do give a most marked preference to the manner of existence which employs their higher faculties."

2) "Few human creatures would consent to be changed into any of the lower animals, for a promise of the fullest allowance of a beast's pleasures;

3) "No intelligent human being would consent to be changed into a fool, no instructed person would be an ignoramus, no person

of feeling and conscience would be selfish and base, even though they should be persuaded that the fool, the dunce, or the rascal is better satisfied with his lot than theirs."

Happiness is not just contentment, because then "the being whose capacities for enjoyment are low, has the greatest chance of having them fully satisfied; and a highly endowed being will always feel that any happiness which he can look for, as the world is constituted, is imperfect."

Most everyone can be happy if he has even one of these: a cultivated mind or much tranquillity or some excitement.

"With much tranquillity, many find they can be content with very little pleasure: with much excitement, many can reconcile themselves to a considerable quantity of pain. There is assuredly no inherent impossibility in enabling even the mass of mankind to unite both; ..."

"A cultivated mind–I do not mean that of a philosopher, but any mind to which the fountains of knowledge have been opened, and which has been taught, in any tolerable degree, to exercise its faculties–finds sources of inexhaustible interest in all that surrounds it; in the objects of nature, the achievements of art, the imaginations of poetry, the incidents of history, the ways of mankind past and present, and their prospects in the future." So most can be happy unless they demand constant kicks.

We need to measure happinesses to act for the greatest. How? [Mill knows you can't turn on your eudaimonometer (happiness meter) and follow the alternative with the greatest reading!] Also, there is the theoretical problem of meshing individual happiness with the general happiness.

Mill adds the "present wretched education, and wretched social arrangements, are the only real hindrance to its being attained by almost all." and "Next to selfishness, the principal cause which makes life unsatisfactory is want of mental cultivation." [Is he implying that education and/or social reform can diminish selfishness itself?]

B. Infinite

Is earthly bliss totally impossible? Bad luck, illness, poverty, neurosis, ugliness, tragedy, stupidity, etc. are pretty formidable obstacles. Even if several of these could be eradicated as thoroughly as smallpox, others would pop up.

Is happiness too much for us? Or are we too much for it? No finite condition will ever satisfy us.

For Pascal, man is an incomprehensible monster, full of paradox, tension, dissatisfaction, contradiction, exaltation. Yet despite our damaged or twisted nature, happiness is there for us: "Happiness is neither without us nor within us. It is in God, both without us and within us."[13]

Augustine cries out "We shall not rest until we rest in Thee." God is the `Ancient Beauty', eternal and unchanging, who alone can fill our hunger for eternal truth and unchanging happiness.[14]

Spinoza says blessedness is intellectual love of God.[15] It includes intuitive science or the advance from adequate knowledge of God to the adequate knowledge of things. God is infinite substance. [By substance, Spinoza means what exists *of* itself and there can be but one substance. For Aristotle, substance is what exists *in* itself, as contrasted to 'accident' which exists in another (e.g. yellow exists in a flower) and there are many substances.] Spinoza's God is everything. What may be conceived as distinct things are in reality attributes of God. Increasing knowledge of God increases being or power which causes joy. The wise are happy and far forward in this infinite advance.

For Sartre, can happiness be possible? The universe has two types of reality: being-in-itself and being-for-itself.[16] A being-in-itself is a thing, like a chair. It has an essence but no openness. It is just and exactly what it is. No more.

Human beings have freedom and potential. Man is ever making himself by his own choices. Man has no essence but is a project in the process of coming to be, pure openness. Yet man is always trying to be a being-in-itself. He wants to be some-*thing*. He wants to turn existence into essence, freedom into fact. But this cannot be, man is condemned to be free. As for the Infinite, Sartre seems to hold that God is a contradictory mix of essence and freedom, but elsewhere he claims that atheism is a choice. Let us look more closely at a few thinkers for whom happiness is a quest for the infinite.

NIETZSCHE

For Nietzsche happiness involves an infinite quest in the sense of infinite as not being bound, breaking all bounds and bonds. Yet his idea of happiness is both godless and bound by death. Nietzsche writes of "transvaluing all values", and of getting "beyond good and evil". For him almost everything we praise and prize is "slave morality" or "frog perspective". His *Die Fröhliche Wissenschaft* translates to Happy Science, but is it a science of happiness? [17] His work is largely a series of pithy attacks on things. And parts of his philosophy tend to destroy other parts. There are many flecks of genius and insight in his work. But even the most brilliant criticism of sculpture does not chisel a thing of beauty.

Could Nietzsche's legacy be to make us ponder: How does happiness stand with pure excitement, adventure; living to the limit with the throttle all the way out; being totally plugged into the moment; being as alive as is possible at the moment -whether or not the moment can stretch to forever?

Jack Kerouac says, "...the only people for me are the mad ones, the ones who are mad to live, mad to talk, mad to be saved, desirous of everything at the same time, the ones who never yawn or say a commonplace thing but burn, burn, burn like fabulous yellow roman candles exploding like spiders across the stars...!" [18]

SANKARA

If happiness is union with God or the One or all-being, it may be beyond 'ordinary experience' but not beyond all possible experience. Can philosophy talk about it even if it can't manufacture it? For Sankara, union with God is direct and total. He takes the words of the Upanishads *tat tvam asi* (thou art that) to be the key understanding. [19] The most sublime and exalted reality-in-itself (Brahma, God) and the innermost point of the individual's being (atman, soul) are the same.

This consciousness (*Cit*) of being (*Sat*) is joy (*Ananda*). Taking the world as multiple or other than God is illusion (*maya*). As a rope on the ground is mistakenly taken to be a snake, so that which is one, is falsely taken to be many. Overcoming this brings release (*moksha*).

There are philosophical difficulties with illusion. Although illusion can explain the rope's not being a snake, can illusion also explain illusion itself? Is it an illusion that we are "illuded"? Sankara calls his teaching *Advaita* (non-dualism, monism). Other Hindu thinkers disagree. Madhva says that while union with God is our joy, identity is not possible. God is opulently blissful and eternal, we can suffer and began to be. Ramanuja takes an intermediate position in his 'modified non-dualism'. These thinkers dispute how God is related us, but not that happiness is to be with God in full joy.

BUDDHISM

Buddhism is often said to be atheistic and its *nirvana* to be annihilation. Indeed nirvana means 'blowing out (a candle)'. But another reading is that nirvana is pure consciousness open to and filled with perfect-being. The word Buddha is from *budh* -to be awake, to be conscious of. [20]

"But now I have seen thee housebuilder, never more shalt thou build this house. The rafters of sin are broken, the ridge-pole of ignorance is destroyed. The fever of craving is past: for my mortal mind is gone to the joy of the immortal NIRVANA." [153,154]

"And the man whose mind, filled with determination, is longing for the infinite NIRVANA, and who is free from sensuous pleasures, is called *uddham soto*, `he who goes upstream', for against the current of passions and worldly life he is bound for the joy of the Infinite. Just as a man who has long been far away is welcomed with joy on his safe return by his relatives, well-wishers and friends; in the same way the good works of a man in his life welcome him in another life, with the joy of a friend meeting a friend on his return." [218-220]

"And when he sees in a clear vision the coming and going of inner events, then he feels the infinite joy of those who see the immortal THAT; the NIRVANA immortal." [374]

"In a fullness of delight and of faith in the teaching of Buddha, the mendicant monk finds peace supreme and, beyond the transience of time, he will find the joy of Eternity." [381]

WESTERN THEOLOGY

For the blessed, Boethius says, God is the "beginning, driver, leader, pathway, end." [21] Some say God is the highest good, but not for us because he does not know us or cannot be touched in any way by us. Today such a notion is rare. Even atheists, generally have in mind a God that would 'fill the bill' for happiness, if he existed.

We focus on two philosophical questions:

1) As finite beings, do we have to change or be changed radically to fit happiness with God? Apart from theology or revelation, a philosophical issue is involved: Are we steady and stable enough to hold happiness even if given it? Or must we be shaped up ('metaphysical fitness') for happiness?

2) What is the relation between the excellences of earthly life and supernatural bliss with God?

What have philosophers done on these?

1) For Thomas Aquinas, God is our happiness and joy. We can have some share in that joy in this life—but life with God is only begun, it is not fulfilled here. Paradise is somehow both a contemplation of and a sharing in God's own life. He brings in ideas beyond the scope of philosophy—the Trinity and the Incarnation. Happiness is more bestowed than earned, he says, quoting Augustine's saying "God was made man that man might be made God." [22]

God is a joy beyond anything we could ever desire. The human self as we find it is so constituted that it can only hold so much. God has to expand human capacities before He fulfills them. Instead of joy flowing into us, we go into Joy.

2) Augustine and Thomas connect Greek philosophical ideas of earthly virtue and bliss with the supernatural joy promised by religion. For example, in almost every case, the action that Aristotle and Augustine/Aquinas would call for is the same. But many religious writers in their zeal to glorify God, 'put down' natural excellences and emphasize what is wrong with man. We let Josef Pieper, a contemporary German philosopher, speak for Thomas and others because he speaks a modern philosophical idiom and gives fresh reasons for ancient ideas.

JOSEF PIEPER

Is happiness more doing the good than having the good? What is the relation between happiness and the love of other persons? Pieper says: [23]

1) We wish to 'have' the whole good. [The mere existence of the good is not enough. The mere existence of the drink does not sate the drinker.] Three things are implied. We have a thirst; it is to have, possess, take, receive etc. something; it is directed to the universal good, not just to a limited part of it. The whole good can't be an infinite parade of successive goods. [Is this what Hobbes thinks we want? But getting the whole family together for Christmas doesn't mean seeing them in different stages.]

2) Love is the indispensable premise of happiness. If one doesn't love then one can't be unhappy, since unhappiness = failure to possess what you love. But one cannot be happy either, since one cannot rejoice in the possession of something unless one loves it.

3) What is chiefly loved (by the will) cannot be love itself (an act of the will).

i) Two reasons are given: a) If our chief thing were an act of the will all we would have to do is will it—shazam! We would have it and so could/would be happy just by willing it so. b) It can be empty just to will an act of the will. A courageous fireman loves the good of others, so he is willing to die to save them. But what if what he loved most was simply "to be a courageous man"? His love would be directed away from the noble object of saving others to a pure state of mind. But then what makes courage great evaporates. It is a good to love oneself and virtue, but this way is empty.

ii) Morality also cannot be our chief aim since morality "makes arrangements for something else". For example, a man has a serious drinking problem. By great inner struggle, friends' help, etc. he gets the problem under control. We and he rejoice in his temperance. But temperance is not a supreme goal, it is for the happiness that opens to a sober life.

iii) The delight and rapture that come from possession of the good is not willed directly, rather the good is. E.g., on the day of the great race, Eric Little strains and yearns to win the race. He does win. He is happy. But what if he got up that morning and said to himself not "I want to win!" but "I want the joy of winning!"? There is something off about that, something neurotic perhaps - which may be why it normally doesn't happen. Happiness and joy are ultimate goodies but as riders on the actuality that brings them. 4)The best form of 'having' is not material possession. We can have something either by becoming it or not becoming it. We 'have' warmth by becoming warm, not by studying thermodynamics in a frozen room. But usually having is not material ingestion. We have a sunset by seeing; we are aware in skiing of the flow, the speed, the snow; fun with friends is in doing and talking but mostly in being together with those we love.

5)There is a close union in the kind of having called knowing. What kind of union? Aristotle says <intellect in knowing a thing> and the <intelligible known content or what is known in the thing> are identical. Also my knowing it and your knowing it are the same. Epistemology is tricky but lets see what this might mean. Take the Pythagorean Theorem $a^2+b^2=c^2$ for any right triangle. Another student might express this as $x^2+y^2=z^2$. Someone might turn the triangle sideways or upside down. To learn, teach, express, retain or recall this mathematical truth we must 'hold it in mind' by some such representation or imagination. The representations are obviously different. What we imagine is different but what we 'intellect' or understand is the same. It must be the same because otherwise it is a different truth-world for each knower. When we think we are animatedly exchanging thoughts about a theorem or a piano or a giraffe, we are actually sliding past each other on different mind tracks. Of course, there is a sense in which we know the same thing or person differently. Our knowledge can be partial like the five blind Hindus and the elephant. Yet even here there is some kernel of overlap, of identity. When we both remember how funny someone was, isn't something 'the same' there with us?

6) "Intuition" is the 'realest' form of knowing. A theorem is abstract, dry, distant. Intuition-presence or insight-union is not discursive. Deep spirited wonder is not like studying for an exam. We know music and color when their chromatic harmonies dwell in us. The proper way to have friends is to be with them. It is this 'resting in the beloved thing', the 'loving attainment of awareness', the intuition of the other, the being-at-one-with the loved reality—

that is the most intense kind of having. In insight-union we are joined with the object and are aware that we are. What the Hindus call Sat-Cit-Ananda, Pieper, like Aristotle and Aquinas, calls contemplation.

7) Is happiness hard or easy? common or rare? Is it a gift from outside or something we produce?

Happiness as earthly contemplation is actually very common, Pieper says. Insights or 'inscapes' come upon us from all over the place when we leave ourselves open to them. The insight may come while waiting for a subway in Brooklyn or hiking around in Brixen; it may be set off by a silly face, an accidental remark or a flower by the road. No matter, it is really an opening to the universal good. We may not be aware of them as inscapes nor connect them to any source.

For Aristotle, contemplation is the intellectual dwelling in the eternal and necessary nonhuman order of the universe. It is enhanced by friends but is not itself an act of friendship. Man cannot be a friend of God.

If, however, this world is the free creation of God, then, in contemplating parts of the world, we are contemplating images and deeds of God. So what an inscape is about is also God. God is the object of which all intuitions are partial adumbrations or incomplete participations. [Recall Plato -in loving any beautiful thing we are really loving Beauty Itself.]

A more direct intuition-presence of God Himself is a gift beyond any earthly effort since God is not a phenomenon to be stumbled upon among his own works. At its highest level contemplation is seeing God - much more like being with a friend than gazing at the stars. It is sublimely and intimately personal. However, since it is a gift, we cannot summon it up at will. Nor can we exhaustively analyze it. The analysis and, *a fortiori*, the achievement of such happiness is beyond philosophy's proof but not its probe. As a gift, can the vision of God also be an activity? Yes, because if a blind man were given sight, he would still see with his own sense of sight.

8) If so much of even earthly fun comes from true seeing and hearing, then whatever jams our space with empty content damages joy. How often meaningless messages, flat sights, grinding

noises war in the rich soulscape that is our true land.
What is the philosophical status of this theory? We do seem to
have an infinite thirst. The thirst doesn't prove or provide the drink.
But if we are made for the Infinite Drink, that does explain the
thirst.

III. A Coda

Philosophers differ about happiness because they differ greatly
about what is and what is most real (metaphysics). Most do put
noble action on the side of happiness and reject base deeds as a
route to any true joy–in this they agree with religion (and common
sense?).

(Unsurprisingly?) many philosophers put happiness in thinking, mental cultivation, learning, conversation–despite huge dis-
agreements about what really exists: Epicurus has odd gods and a
material mind; Aristotle has an immaterial principle and a God in
splendid isolation; Mill is an empiricist who doesn't bring in God
at all; the thought of Augustine, Aquinas, and Sankara is drenched
in God.

If thinking is a large part of happiness, thinking-into and
truthing-out about happiness is itself happy-making (felicific).

If 'ordinary people' were asked at random about happiness
would they give answers like our philosophers? Aristotle feels the
ordinary person is forever beneath the higher things. Spinoza sharply
contrasts the wise man to the unthinking mob. But is there really
this huge permanent gap? Or is the gulf largely due to individual
woes and the general woes of an age or society? Poor, broken,
confused and humiliated...

If some woes are artificially induced by "philosophical mistakes" they may be curable by clear thinking.

We suggest two: 1) A confusion of work and play, making and
doing. 2) 'Busyness business' which fills the space and time opened
up by technology with yet more technology instead of leisure–the
locus of thankfulness and glory. [see our Metaphysical Tools].

It is not the business of philosophy to preach. But since happiness is both an abstract theme and a concrete goal, philosophy encourages us to put aside for a few moments any harried informa-

tion or vexation about how things are or what to do and pull up a great wonder: 'why is there something rather than just nothing?!' or 'how unfathomable that I exist, that you exist?!' Don't just hear these questions as passing trains, ride with them awhile. Dostoyevski said we are all happy if we but knew it. [24]

IV. Footnotes and References

1. Jefferson, Thomas, *Declaration of Independence.*

2. *Encyclopedia of Philosophy*, (Paul Edwards ed., New York, Macmillan, 1967) p.413-414

3. Aristotle, *Nicomachean Ethics.* Books I and X are the key ones here. Direct citations are by the Bekker numbers, *Basic Works of Aristotle*, (New York, Random House, 1970, tr. W.D. Ross).

4. Sartre, John Paul, *Being and Nothingness* (tr. Hazel E. Barnes, New York, Washington Square Press, 1953). His philosophical ideas are suffused throughout plays and essays.

5. Epicurus, *Letters, Principal Doctrines and Vatican Sayings* (tr. Russel Geer), Indianapolis, Bobbs Merrill 1964. See also the poem of his Roman disciple, Lucretius, *De Rerum Natura*, On the Nature of Things, (Loeb Classical Library, Cambridge MA, 1975).

6. Kant, Immanuel, *Foundations of the Metaphysics of Morals* (tr. Lewis White Beck), Indianapolis, Bobbs Merrill, 1959. For the 'moral argument' see also *Critique of Practical Reason* (tr. Lewis White Beck), New York 1960) and *Religion within the Limits of Reason Alone* (tr. T.M. Greene and H.H. Hudson), Harper&Row, New York 1960.

7. Sophocles, *Oedipus at Colonus*, line 1222-1223.

8. Marx, Karl, *Das Kapital,* (ed. Friedrich Engels, Regnery-Gateway, Chicago, 1967). Abridged by Serge Levitsky. *The Communist Manifesto* (tr. Samuel Moore), Regnery- Gateway, Chicago, 1954.

9. Hobbes, Thomas, *Leviathan* (ed. Michael Oakeshott, Collier-Macmillan, New York, 1971). Prufer, Thomas, *verbal communication.*

10. Epictetus, *Moral Discourses, Enchiridion and Moral Fragments,* (tr. Elizabeth Carter), Everyman's Library, London, 1966.

The originals were put down by Epictetus' disciple, Arrian. The quote is from Enchiridion XVII.

11. Aristotle, 1177b26-1178a2.

12. Mill, John Stuart, *Utilitarianism,* Everyman's Library, London, p. 8-12. See also *Great Traditions in Ethics*, Albert, Denise and Peterfreund, Wadsworth Publ. Belmont CA, 1984.

13. Pascal, Blaise, *Pensées,* (Great Books, vol. 33), #465. The Pensées are numbered by different systems.

14. Augustine, *Confessions,* Loeb Classical Library, Cambridge MA, 1968, Book I, p.1.

15. Spinoza, Baruch, *Ethics,* Part V, Prop. XXXII-XXXVI, p.262-265 in *Works of Spinoza*, (tr. R. Elwes) Dover, New York 1951.

16. Sartre, *Being and Nothingness.*

17. Nietzsche, Fredrich, *The Gay Science* (tr. Walter Kaufmann, Random House, New York, 1974). See also *Beyond Good and Evil, The Genealogy of Morals*, etc. While Nietzsche gives a fairly consistent general impression, we find it hard to frame his ideas into a general system.

18. Kerouac, Jack, *On The Road,*Penguin Books,NY,1959,p.8

19. Sankara, The *Vedanta Sutras of Badarayana* with the Commentary by Sankara (tr George Thibaut), Dover, New York 1962, p.31-35. The quote is from*Khandogya Upanishad* VI 8,7. See also Radhakrishnan, S. and Moore, C. eds. *A Source Book in Indian Philosophy*, Princeton NJ, 1957,pp.506-572. Many Westerners take extreme monism to be the Hindu position. For Madhva see *Sri tattva muktavali*, The Krsna Institute, Culver City, CA, 1988.

20. *The Dhammapada* (tr. Juan Mascaro), Penguin Classics, London 1973. Citations are by verse number.

21. Boethius, *The Consolation of Philosophy*, (tr. S.J. Tester) Loeb Classical Library, Cambridge MA, 1978, p.275.

22. Thomas Aquinas, *Summa Theologica*, Pt. III q1 a3 quotes Augustine and says happiness is bestowed on us by Christ's humanity. Pt.II-II q.28 a3 says we go into Joy.

23. Pieper, Josef, *Happiness and Contemplation* (tr. Richard and Clara Winston), Pantheon Books, New York 1958. The book is unfortunately out of print. Teutoleges (readers of German) may try *Glück und Kontemplation*, Kösel-Verlag, München. This summary

and some examples are mine. The merit belongs to Pieper. I take
the blame for distortions/misunderstandings.

24. Dostoyevski, Fyodor, *The Possessed* (tr. Constance
Gannett), Random House, New York 1936, cited from Barrett,
William, *The Illusion of Technique*, Doubleday, New York 1979,
p.377.

The Great Books of the Western World has an index on happiness (vol. 2 p.695-710). For the Arabic, Oriental, etc. thinkers, an
encyclopedia article may be a good place to start. Then follow up
under individual names. Many of their works remain untranslated.

V. Questions

1) If two people differ on happiness, is there anyway this can
be resolved? Practically: Can a third person see more clearly? If
not, why are there mediators, counselors, etc.? Theoretically: Is
there any way of telling who is more correct? Does changing one's
mind, conversion, regret, etc. have anything to tell us here? Can
we measure different notions against something objective -e.g.,
human nature, science, etc.

2) If happiness lies mainly in avoiding something, what does
that tell us about human nature or existence in general?

3) If happiness is "living to the hilt", doesn't this behavior usually hurt others (and oneself)? Can life be an exciting adventure
while enhancing others rather than hurting them? Give practical
and theoretical suggestions.

4) Do you accept the axiom that everyone wants to be happy?
If so, why are so few people happy? Or are most people happy? If
you reject the axiom, could someone who is now happy want to
stop being happy? Elaborate.

5) Kant seems to identify happiness with satisfaction and this
has been criticized. But if it isn't satisfaction, what is it?

6) A corollary of the Plato/Aristotle view that happiness lies in
virtue is that the "vicious man" cannot be happy. What if he says
he is? Comment.

7) If it is possible that a person be granted happiness without
deserving it (even being a scoundrel!), what problems are raised?

8) If just to exist (or to reflect on this) is the main ingredient of happiness, shouldn't people be a lot closer to happiness than we find them? Or does existence have to be filled or transformed in some way?

9) Are some groups happier than others? What does empirical science have to contribute here?

10) Thinkers from Aristotle to Mill put happiness on the side of contemplation or "menticulture". How would you respond to one who thinks: a) it isn't worth the effort b) it is too cold and abstract c) it has nothing to do with love.

11) What is the relation of love to happiness?

12) Does happiness lie more in personal relations than in anything else?

13) How do the last two items relate to a personal God?

14) If happiness is infinite can it be reached? Can we attain it only if it is given us?

15) The chapter began by asking some questions. Now give your reasoned answer: a) Is happiness something we have or do or are? b) Is it easy or hard? c) Is it in our power or does it come from without? d) Do we have to change to be happy?

Ta tria tauta meidzon de tauton e agape.
Corinthians, I, 13, 13

LOVE

I. Introduction

II. Plato

III. Aristotle

IV. Jesus

V. Sigmund Freud

VI. Carson McCullers

VII. Vladimir Solovyov

VIII. Theoretical Problems:
   A. Selfish or Selfless
   B. Other Problems

IX. A Question; A Thought Experiment;
   A Gathering

X. Footnotes and References

XI. Questions

I. Introduction

Love is a popular theme, possibly too popular for clear discussion. Many people think of only one kind of love e.g., romantic love or sexual love. Here we are looking for what is in all kinds of love, the essence of love.

What words should we use? Philosophy's founding fathers, the Greeks, had three main words for love: *eros*–desire or yearning; *philia*–friendship love; and *agape*–the word the early Christian church used for the love of God. In the Bible at least 52 different Greek, Hebrew and Aramaic words are used in connection with love, according to Gerhard Kittel's *Bible Key Words* [J.R. Coates tr. Harper & Row]. This allows one to make many fine points, but since here we look for the overarching sense or common thread in all love, we feel this is a disadvantage not an advantage. The reality analogously common to all kinds of love of all kinds of beings for all kinds of beings does better with one central word to point with. English love; German Liebe; French amour; Portuguese, Latin, Spanish amor; Chinese ài; Italian amore; Russian lyubov.

Some questions: Is love one thing? Is it better to love than not to love? (Doesn't love bring suffering?) Is love the best thing? How must it be qualified and/or controlled? What should be loved? How is loving related to knowing? Is it better to love friends or enemies? What do theories of love say about God? What does the fact of love tell us about human reality and reality in general? Is love a necessary condition of human existence, a sort of gravity that works on us from within or without? At an other extreme, can it be an arbitrary or whimsical election or commitment made in inner isolation? What is the relation between love and happiness?

Some of these questions may be unanswerable if they are badly put. Let's first look at what love is.

II. Plato

In the *Phaedrus*,[1] Plato defends love against arguments that the loveless enjoyment of others is more rewarding and efficient than

the entanglements and sufferings of love. There he calls love "divine madness". In the *Symposium* Plato's makes these central points:
1) Love is love of, love of something, love of x (where x = any loved object).
2) We seek to be united with what we love.
3) The love of something (x), is always of the good in x, the beautiful in x, never of the ugly, harmful etc. in x.
4) Love always goes beyond or overshoots, the particular things it may start with. This sets up a progression or dynamic or hierarchy in love.
5) Therefore, love is most aimed at (or the lover is most drawn to) the most beautiful -Beauty Itself.
Evidences/Arguments for these:
1) A simple logical point. Love is not a being, it is a relation to a being.
2) The union varies with the object loved. We are one with a sunset in seeing it, with wine in drinking it, with a theorem in thinking it, with our friends in being together with them. But in each case to love is to seek union.
3) If I love a woman who is ugly, I don't love her because she is ugly (if I could cure the ugliness I would), but because of other qualities. Note here that love has a cause -beauty or goodness- which pulls on a person, like gravity.
4) and 5) If you like to see a good race, you'll love the greatest sprint ever run! If you like this rotgut wine, you'll love this fine Gallic vintage! If you like this case of beauty, you'll love Beauty Itself!
[Plato says that whenever many things are truly called by one name (e.g. horse, circle, red), then there exists a pure and complete instance of that one (the Horse Itself, the Circle Itself, The Red Itself).] Leave aside whether Beauty Itself has a real independent existence. Isn't it true that, if love involves being drawn or attracted to the beauty in things, then the greater the beauty, the more one is attracted. The greater magnet pulls harder.
Since Plato uses eros (yearning, desire), he must say that love is of what one does not possess. We need no such qualifier. You can love what you have but not yearn for it. He also must leave alone love of self and love of something 'for its own sake' since one can

hardly yearn for oneself or love wine for its own sake. These limits are built into the type of love he is discussing (desire), not love itself.

What/Who is Beauty Itself? Can Beauty love or only be loved? The answer does not seem obvious. One who was willing to die for freedom could be called a friend of freedom. But is freedom the kind of thing that can love you back? On the other hand, Christian Platonists identify Beauty with God.

III. Aristotle

Aristotle's word is philia -which we also translate as like or liking. A friend is someone who likes you. He describes how friendship actually occurs and connects his theories of friendship and happiness.[2] He does assume that objective beauty and goodness exist in the world and in human thought and action.

There are three types of friendship depending on its 'basis': a) utility b) pleasure c) excellence. The first two are deficient as friendships but there is nothing evil in them and they are very common.

a) I go to a doctor for a series of monthly treatments that last two years. While there I get to know him somewhat and enjoy talking to him. However, when the treatments are over I no longer drop by just for some good conversation. There is no note of exploitation or 'using' the other person. I recommend him to other people and he does the same for me. It is simply that the friendship only goes to a certain length. If I should see him our conversation might pick up quite animatedly. I could invite him over. But just because I don't, doesn't mean there never was any friendship at all.

b) You go snorkeling with a circle of people. You enjoy this bunch but primarily as doing these things with them. [You don't have to separate all this out in your mind, of course.] If your or their interest in snorkeling ceases, the friendships dry up as well. Again, this doesn't mean you never really liked these people, but only that your fondness did not reach beyond a certain depth. There needn't be any hurt or resentment of any kind. The friendship fades away because the enjoyment it floated on is gone. You are free to keep up the friendships but then they would move to a different level.

Today, some feel hypocritical calling these friendships at all. True, they are not friendships in the full sense. But we should not think of them as always phony or exploitative.

c) True friendship is the love of another person for the excellence in him/her and for his/her own sake. The more excellent a person is the more he can give and receive true friendship. The noble type of person loves better because he loves the better things. He is also a more fitting 'object' to be loved because he is excellent. Therefore only the good can fully and truly have and be friends. [Remember: a noble person is one who loves excellence regardless of what he actually possesses.]

You can love someone in a defective way and in spite of their defects, but both diminish friendship.

We confine ourselves to few points.

i) Do we love what is good in itself or what is good for us? For the excellent person these tend to be the same because he 'lines himself up' with the truly good. When the noble are friends, their friendship is solidly rooted in each other's real excellence and so is least liable to change, most to be trusted.

ii) Here and elsewhere in his philosophy, Aristotle distinguishes between a mere state, aptitude or disposition of something and the exercise or activity or actuality of that something. A sleeping violinist is still a violinist but he is most violinist when he is actually playing. So with friendship. Friends delight in being together. That doesn't mean you can't have an absent friend. But the actuality of friendship is eclipsed if you can't "do the friend thing" because there is no contact.

iii) Friendship is more in loving than in being loved. Aristotle notes the paradox that a mother loves her child more than she is loved. [Paradoxical -children should be more grateful and hence more loving.] He denies any paradox.[3] "The reason is that all desire and love existence, and that we exist by activity (i.e. by living and doing). The handiwork is in a sense, the producer in activity; so he loves his handiwork, because he loves existence." (1168a5-7) So a poet loves his poems. So a mother loves her child.

[A digression. Hegel[4] uses the art work to say something else. The finished art work stands as a reality on its own (a being-in-itself) over and against the artist (a being-for-itself). The artist's inner reality changes but the art work does not change (like looking at old photos perhaps!) Hegelian alienation is interior and spiritual. Once something is done or made, it fixes as historical deed or external product, unlike the flux of its spiritual maker.

Who's right? Is doing/making alienating or unfolding, estrangement or fruition? The answer may depend on one's metaphysics. Here a contrast is between being-in-itself/being-for-itself (Hegel) and potential/actual (Aristotle). For Hegel, alienation can be overcome by the dialectic called *aufheben* involving the triple: thesis, antithesis, synthesis. This digression shows how hard it is to use even a simple example without bringing in almost everything.]

iv) The self is another friend. The noble person is his own best friend. All the essentials are there: goodness, being together, delight in the same things, for one's own sake, wish well to, equality, awareness, longlastingness.

v) The friend is another self. Elsewhere Aristotle argues that the highest activity and the greatest happiness is contemplation. By which he means chiefly thinking about the necessary and eternal truths involved in the way reality is. Contemplation is spoken of as "something divine present in us" and as perhaps "too high for man". Friends help. Their insights guide, pollinate or reinforce our own. Our music is amplified, echoed, sustained, filtered and reverberated. The chill and loneliness of solitary thought is warmed in a comity of wisdom and wonder.

vi) Friendship involves equality though not a rigid mathematical kind. He says, "...for much can be taken away and friendship remain, but when one party is removed to a great distance, as God is, friendship is no more. This is the origin of the question whether friends really wish for their friends the greatest goods, e.g. that of being gods; since then they will no longer be friends." (1159a)

[Contrast: To Christians, the Incarnation is not only for a double negation (remove sin). It is the capstone and epiphany of love: "You are my friends" and "I call you friends" (John 15, 14-16).]

IV. Jesus

[We include Jesus here because there is a doctrine of love and reasonings about it in the Gospels.[5]] The teaching of Jesus centers on God's love for us. It is more about being loved than about loving. Here we extract a small part of this teaching and put it in philosophical dress.

1) The creator God exists. 2) God loves us. 3) In response, love God, each other, thyself.

Arguments or evidences:

1) Creation itself is assumed. But there are some for whom origin from God is a philosophical topic. If so, then whatever love that origin implies is also.

2) However, Jesus does argue that God loves us. He feeds the birds and clothes the lilies (Mt 6,28, Lk 12,28), so a fortiori, He loves us and we are to trust Him. [Isn't it implicit that since humans are 'realer' than birds and flowers, we are the fruit of a deeper love?]

3) Response is the key word. It reverses Plato's direction. For Plato, love is the impetus drawing us upward to pure beauty and goodness. To love fully is to climb a steep mountain. Jesus preaches a love that cascades down the mountain. He teaches that God 'firstmost' loves us (the prodigal son; the vine and the branches; love one another as I have loved you). Self and others are prodigously enhanced when viewed as the intimate family of God.

What kind of love does God keep for us in the iconic instruction of Jesus? We find four faces—a quaternity:

1) taking-care-of, shepherding, parental 2) creative, generative 3) royal, loyal friendship 4) ecstatic union. [Brotherhood is a fifth face emphasized by Dostoyevski.] The paternal/parental face is the aspect most emphasized by Jesus. A father runs to his far off son (Lk 15,20). Creation is like human fecund love in that it brings forth beings to the bright coasts of life. It is an act of pure generosity not one required to complete or perfect God. As made in the image of God, we have thereby one key characteristic of ordinary friendships -likeness. But divine friendship is a surprise piece of good-news, an 'ontological lagniappe' that raises us above our natural station. A special gift which releases us from the sort of limits

that one might, like Aristotle, expect to be our lot.

Ecstatic union with God is imaged at Cana where our water is turned to divine wine. The Moslem Sufis also 'image' God by wine. This last is the divine love for Christian mystics[6] (Teresa of Avila, John of the Cross, etc.) and for mystics outside Christianity (Rumi, Caitanya, etc.). The Last Supper prayer: "May they all be one, Father, may they be one in us, as you are in me and I am in you, ..." (Jn 17,21).

How can images imagine the love of God? The new wine in us that bursts the old skins, presumably calls for new words as well. The doctrine does not remain with the descriptive or declarative, it is always yoked to the imperative: Loveback.

The Bible uses concrete parables to show, rather than abstract propositions to state, what God is like. For Thomas, the best philosophical name for God is *esse subsistens*, the subsisting to-be; sheer, complete and unbounded actuality.

[Given such a notion of God, an argument can be made to the notion of His love.] If God is not lacking, He does not need to create. If He does not need to create, His creating is an act of pure generosity. Such a God is superworthy of our love and superfree in His loving.

V. Freud

Freud[7] says all kinds of love are rooted in one impulse (libido). And he says that puts him with Plato and Paul. "Libido is an expression taken from the theory of the emotions. We call by that name the energy (regarded as a quantitative magnitude, though not at present actually measurable) of those instincts which have to do with all that may be comprised under the word love. The nucleus of what we mean by love naturally consists (and this is what is commonly called love and what the poets sing of) in sexual love with sexual union as its aim. But we do not separate from this - what in any case has a share in the name love -on the one hand, self-love, and on the other, love for parents and children, friendship, and love for humanity in general, and also devotion to concrete objects and abstract ideas."

Normally "these instincts force their way toward sexual union, but in other circumstances they are diverted from this aim or prevented from reaching it". The army and the church; psychosis and neurosis; Watteau and Giotto; the pilgrimage to Canterbury and the journey to the moon - all are explained as the expressions and suppressions of love (that's not amazing). And this wonder-worker love is a measureable block of energy (that's amazing!) -see our Reductionism.

VI. Carson McCullers

Philosophers usually prefer to go after the truth in a direct and logical way -building a case, defending premises as they go. Novels are stories, not philosophical tracts. They are to be enjoyed, not argued with. Yet there is much philosophy in certain novels. The novelist can build to the truth with little parts, no one of which need be the whole truth nor perhaps even wholly true. She puts faces and facets together like a grasshoppers eye. Each ommatidium (simple eye) holds a small dispersed part truth. We must do the focusing.

In *The Heart is a Lonely Hunter*,[8] Mick Kelly is a 12-year old whose family runs a boarding house. Every Sunday she and three others come to visit a deaf tenant, John Singer.

Restless electricity pulses through these four: Dr. Benedict Copeland -the strong true purpose of justice especially for the Negro; Jake Blount -to awaken even a few to the Red gospel in the South; Biff the cafe owner -keeping the cafe open all night for no special reason; Mick -eager, bright and quick "Sometimes this fellow's (Mozart's) music was like little colored pieces of crystal candy and other times it was the softest saddest thing she'd ever imagined about." (p.29)

They are happy and peaceful when they see Singer. The three men feel he is the only person who understands them. Mick listens to the radio in his room. Singer is kind and intelligent. He's sure to have coffee out for his visitors.

While they find a haven in him, Singer thinks constantly of Antonapoulos, another mute who was sent away a year ago. He wants to tell him all the things that had come about and how he had been left in an alien land. About Antonapoulos himself? His only interests are food, drink or sleep.

What holds all this together? Love. Biff, Dr. Copeland, Mick and Blount love Singer who loves Antonapoulos who loves food. And Mick is enthralled by Mozart and Beethoven.

Each loves or is fascinated. But two things are made over-clear: 1) The people don't have the qualities they are loved for. 2) Love is not reciprocated.

Is love, then, simply broadcasting or projecting? A beam or call goes into the unhearing darkness. Other people are at most a surface for the projection to land on.

But is there no connection between the loving and the loved? Mick is a sympathique kid. Singer is kind, receptive. The boarding house is a place of real life.

Is love fascination? *Fascinare* -to bewitch, enchant, cast a spell. But no character ever tries to do anything to make themselves loveable. Antonopoulos never shows a good quality. Singer listens, not to please, but because he really is kind and because it relieves the boredom and absence-ache.

This is more accurate: To love = to be fascinated by. We take someone else as raw material and then we wrap thought and emotion about that someone (like a pearl is spun around a grain of sand?).

Love is active. It is not the beauty in the object that draws the lover to it (à la Plato). It is the beauty we put into the object -I think of a kid dragging an ugly doll around, putting into it all sorts of wonderful qualities that no one else can manage to detect.

We are drenched with inwardness, a thing that can lie dormant or come alive. Love is this inwardness full, alive. When dormant, we are empty and in time. When we come alive, time is overcome. The metronome of love is "stopped time". Singer can't remember the time before he had ever known his friend -those days seem unreal to him.

But when awakened: For Mick "The music did not take a long time or a short time. It did not have anything to do with time going by at all." (p.100) and "This summer was different. All the time she was excited. In the morning she couldn't wait to get out of bed and start for the day. And at night she hated like hell to have to sleep again." (p.82)

Love is the soul coming awake, expanding, exploding, imploding. To be with or even potentially with the object that catalyzes the awakening is enough. Restlessness of spirit precedes the existential explosion. It isn't an itch one can grow out of. It is the great waiting to be real, the caterpillar waiting to be a butterfly.

Mick's inwardness explodes when she accidentally hears Beethoven's Third Symphony on the radio. "Then the music started. ...Like God strutting in the night. ...This was her, Mick Kelly, walking in the daytime and by herself at night. In the hot sun and in the dark with all her plans and feelings." (p.100) If to focus we must find a formula, let's say that love is the actuality of the inner world. A person comes to be instead of merely dragging his existence along. The outside comes to be real instead of just being there. Time stops.

But love is not self-actualizing, not self-caused. No one brings himself to this state. There must be some loved object, no matter how inappropriate. When love becomes impossible, because the beloved is beyond access, the lover collapses. Singer commits suicide after he finds that Antonapoulos has died. The others fall apart when Singer dies. For Mick there was the inner room. Foreign countries and music were in the inner room. Ordinary people and activities were in the outer room. After Singer dies and Mick has to drop school to work at Woolworth's -"It was like the inner room was locked somewhere away from her. A very hard thing to understand." (p.301)

Doesn't the fascination bubble have to burst sooner or later, if what it is made up of doesn't exist? Must the lover be broken on the facts of existence? Is McCullers' vision one of only deformity and despair?[9]

Let us venture what may be an extention to her theory. Her characters never lose interest. They don't turn love off. The collapse of hope, not love, brings Singer to suicide and closes Mick's room.

When Mick first heard Beethoven's Third: "Now she felt good. She whispered some words out loud: `Lord forgiveth me, For I knoweth not what I do.' Why did she think of that?" Mick doesn't know because "Everybody in the past few years knew there wasn't any real God." (p.101)

Why does she think of that? Is McCullers' notion of love open to the possibility that if there were an eternal object of fascination hanging around, then there's hope and keeping on -forever excited, like Mick was that summer.

Ontological Loneliness

In *The Member of the Wedding*, McCullers develops another notion. Again the protagonist is a young girl, Frankie, a.k.a. F. Jasmine Addams. She had planned to go off with her brother on his honeymoon and is hurt they left without her:
"The long hundred miles did not make her sadder and make her feel more far away than the knowing that they were them and both together and she was only her ... she knew and almost said aloud: they are the we of me." (p.35)
We use a distinction made much of by Heidegger[10] to suggest two kinds of loneliness: ontic and ontological. Ontic is what has to do with beings, with particulars, situations; ontological has to do with being or being as a whole.
Loneliness at a dance is ontic. It might go away if someone wanted to dance with you.
Ontological loneliness is this: "Doesn't it strike you strange that I am I, and you are you? I am F. Jasmine Addams. And you are Berenice Sadie Brown. And we can look at each other, and touch each other, and stay year in and year out in the same room. Yet always I am I and you are you. And I can't ever be anything else but me, and you can't ever be anything else but you." (p.95)
Boethius put it in one of his famous definitions: A person is an incommunicable individual rational substance.[11] Love leads from the I to the We. It awakens interest. Even when the lover is ignored, he is not lonely.
Love assuages or even overcomes ontic loneliness. But isn't it helpless against the fact "I am I and always and only I" -the metaphysical solitary confinement we call ontological loneliness?
Berenice says, "The point is that we all caught. And we try in one way or another to widen ourself free. ...We go around trying one thing or another, but we caught anyhow."
F. Jasmine wonders, "But what is it all about? People loose and at the same time caught. Caught and loose. All these people and you

don't know what joins them up. There's bound to be some sort of reason and connection. Yet somehow I can't seem to name it. I don't know." (p.99)

If there is an infinite moat about each of us, all the projects or projections imaginable will not span it. How does it stand with 'ontological loneliness'? Is it even a problem?

I see four possible stances:

1) All is depliest one, and therefore the experience of being separate is an illusion. [Sankara, Parmenides]

2) We are truly separate, but that's OK, that's just natural. Only overwrought persons or neurotics are troubled. A sign of maturity is not to be affected by this -so some psychologists think.

3) Loneliness is ontological and it makes a need, a huge hunger. But it cannot be overcome. For some existentialists, it is our condition to be wanting a unity that cannot be.

4) It is real and makes a need, but it can be overcome. This pulls in a realm of being bigger than human selfhood, to which we can, in being joined, be joined to others. A bridge over the whirlpool of separateness. God?!

So again philosophy's chief themes intertwine. What is said about God or human nature selects what may be said about happiness, love or even time. Yet philosophy is not a matter of taking stands, but of staking our thought where the truth lies and making our stand there, in that land.

VII. Vladimir Solovyov

Like McCullers, Vladimir Solovyov[12] thinks of love as a hyperreal state of being; like Freud he starts with biology.

He begins *The Meaning of Love* with a biological claim: Fish and flies reproduce more than we do and feel less love. So reproduction can't be the only thing that love is about. Instead "The meaning and worth of love, as a feeling, is that it really forces us, with all our being, to acknowledge for another the same absolute central significance which, because of the power of our egoism, we are conscious of only in our selves. Love is important not as one of our feelings, but as the transfer of all our interest in life from ourselves to another, as the shifting of the very center of our personal lives.

This is characteristic of every kind of love, but predominately of sexual love; it is distinguished from other kinds of love by greater intensity, by a more engrossing character, and by the possibility of more complete overall reciprocity." (p.51)

Despite the term 'sexual love', 'romantic love' captures the sense better. Physical expression is not required; the love may be unrequited; it may end tragically or soon. His examples include Don Quixote and Romeo and Juliet. Though the one in love may see in the other what no one else can see, love is not an illusion. Rather the highest task of love "is already marked out beforehand in the very feeling of love itself, which inevitably and prior to any kind of realization, introduces its object into the sphere of absolute individuality, sees it in ideal light, and has faith in its absoluteness." (p.58)

The lover sees the beloved in an ideal way. And the task of love is to transform the real into the ideal. This is a huge task. Love cannot achieve perfection and immortality if it remains limited to one person. The task becomes 'to restore the image of God in the living object of his love' and in himself, and in all creation. (p.86)

One falls in love with an individual. One who has fallen in love is without the carapace of egoism. He is vulnerable, but it is a good vulnerability. An armadillo without its shell is quite helpless, but for humans this is the beginning of true growth. The exoskeleton of egoism chokes us off from reality. Love breaks us out of its straight jacket. Falling-in-love comes upon us and changes us. Having found treasure outside of ourselves, we are on the qui vive for all treasure. Love bonds us to all being.

There are many other theories. Spinoza[13] says "Love is joy accompanied by the idea of an external cause." [But what if it brings suffering?] Other systems make love impossible -we are greedy, violent or locked in our own private worlds.[14]

VIII. Problems with Love

Two heavy problems lie across our path. One is why we love - and the challenge is that our love is either selfish or altruistic. Gross or outlandish. The other is what we love - and the challenge is that our love is of only the exterior. Inadequate or cold. The discussion itself is heavy, so if these are not issues to you, you may want to skip ahead.

A. Selfish or Selfless

Is every love painted either selfish or selfless? Must we worry whether we deepdown love for the right reason? The problem assails us from all sides.

Nietzsche, Swinburne and others attack "Christian love" as revelling in suffering; secretly triumphing in deformity and death; a flower of the resentment the weak have for the strong; the enemy of fun, excitement, wild joy, true bigness.

Swinburne writes in the *Hymn to Proserpine*,[15]

"Thou hast conquered, O pale Galilean; the world has grown
grey from thy breath;
We have drunken of things Lethean, and fed on the
fullness of death."

In the *Virtue of Selfishness*, Ayn Rand claims "...love is the spiritual payment given in exchange for the personal, selfish pleasure which one man derives from the virtues of another man's character." (p.44)

From the 'other side', some religious writers,[16] claim that any sort of natural yearning or love is worthless for one seeking purity of heart. Others, even without religious reference, think actions must be altruistic to be authentic.

Can this difficulty be solved by being dissolved? What are some key notions associated with each?

Selfish love: is only for one's own good; suppresses reality of the loved in comparison to the self; puts self first and appropriates object into one's self. Selfless love: for the sake of the other; strips off any element of 'gain'; not a natural impetus; enhances the other; suppresses the self.

But do we actually experience this split? A friend of mine, Kevin McDonald asks "Am I less myself, when I'm with the girl I love?" This dichotomy doesn't seem right. But because this notion is so prevalent, we give five ways in which it might be undermined.

1) We do not experience love as either an emptying out of self or of other. Kevin McDonald is right. The self is enhanced and the other is enhanced.

2) Heidegger[17] goes behind the division between subject and object. His context is different from ours, but his thought may help us here.

A man nailing a board is not conscious of himself as subject and the hammer as object. He sees through the hammer to the task he is doing or perhaps he is day-dreaming about something. The hammer has the reality proper to instruments, which Heidegger calls *Zuhandenheit*, ready-to-hand.

Should the handle break or the head come off, the carpenter's focus shifts to the hammer as a hammer, as an object of some sort which should have properties of a certain kind, etc. This kind of reality he calls *Vorhandenheit*, present-at-hand.

Zuhandenheit is more primordial than Vorhandenheit. The world 'at first go' doesn't come divided into subjects and objects such that we then have a terrible puzzle to put the pieces together. We are always-already-involved.

Similarly, *Mitsein,* being-together-with-others is more primordial than isolated and calculated responses. Rigid barriers are easily 'deconstructed' if their construction was illusory in the first place. Nishida Kitaro,[18] a modern Japanese philosopher, says that a poet's viewing a flower is a pure experience prior to the subjectivity of the poet and the objectivity of the flower.

3) Aristotle might claim that this dilemma (you are either selfish or altruistic) arises because we often weigh the lesser thing as greater. Let's see how this goes.

Suppose I give money to feed war victims (choice A) rather than buy a new car (choice B). The common view is that this is a selfless act. But Aristotle would analyze it this way: I choose A over B. A=myself as a generous person but without a new car and the war victims as having food; B=myself as small-souled or stingy but as having a new car and the war victims as going hungry.

The ordinary view puts material goods ahead of character or virtue. So it finds me taking the lesser part for myself. This quixotic behavior is then explained as selfless.

But in either case self is involved. Choice A involves a richer self if you weigh things differently. And this is backed up by experience -one who acts this way often feels an enriched sense of his own being.

Of course, there could be hypocrisy if you pretend to care for someone in a way you don't -you use the poor to show your benevolence while running for President. But is such a person really fooling himself or plagued by profound doubts?

4) Joseph Ratzinger,[19] writes "...a being is more itself the more it is open, the more it is in relationship. And that in turn will lead us to realize that it is the man who makes himself open to all being in its wholeness and in its Ground, and becomes thereby a 'self' who is truly a person."

Self increases as relationship increases. This implies (if yet another barbaric neologism can be forgiven) that love is self-full, neither selfish nor selfless.

5) The main senses we give love involve some kind of union or bridge between people (or from a person to a thing). To take what overarches the self and force it back into the self approaches a contradiction. It makes the unifying factor not a unifying factor. This is like insisting that the glue binding two surfaces joins one or the other but not both.

B. Other Problems

In Robert Johann's *The Meaning of Love*,[20] three more problems emerge. Johann says one loves something either for one's own sake (desire love) or for its own sake (direct love). [We see deep paradoxes with this division itself.]

If you love wine, you love to drink wine; if you love a sports car, you imagine yourself flying around turns or impressing friends. You don't wish well to wine, you wouldn't give up your life for your sports car. We desire the object to be united with us, to be possessed, enjoyed by us.

In desire love, I am in some way incomplete and the object when 'added' to me, enhances me, makes me more actual. Desire for knowledge fits this desciption precisely. If you love chemistry, you want to annex the knowledge of chemicals to yourself. You are a potential chemist, in potency toward this knowledge. As you learn, you become an actual chemist. Another way of putting it: You (as you are now) love you (as you will be knowing chemistry). Technically then, desire involves a self that would go from potency to act.

We saw desire love criticized as only self love. If we add that, e.g., we don't really love wine, we only love the effect wine has on us, this looks even more narcissistic.

But Johann goes on to a deeper problem.

I order an Ayinger beer. I am called out of the room. Someone mistakenly drinks my beer. An identical one replaces it. When I come back I don't mind, even if I do notice.

In this kind of love what we actually love is the type, form, essence of a thing and not the individual or what is unique to this particular thing. The proof is that it can be replaced by its like.

But this won't do for love of a person. Try it out! Try a metaphysical gambit -tell your belle that you love her as an instance of female beauty. Top it off by adding that her identical twin elicits an identical response.

Do we "see past" the person loved? Do we love only the `outside' of another? This is an issue, not of why we love, but of what we love. Even with direct love, don't we have to know a little about a thing in order to love it? Love is somewhat dependent on, even if not controlled by, knowledge. But how does knowing go? We apprehend what is external and understand what is universal. We learn the general properties of circles. I know the taste of a beer as one of a kind. My awareness does not touch what is interior and particular. [Duns Scotus says each thing has a unique property called its *haecceity* (thisness) but whether this solves the problem is not clear.] Leaving this aside, at least two other problems emerge. Is direct love even possible? Can we love something so disinterestedly that any kind of union with it is not even sought. Can we take interest in or love something that has no relation to us? Mustn't it then lie entirely outside our own realm, our *"ontosphere"*? And if so, isn't the whole thing so abstract and dry that it's hardly real?

So we want to say that love has something to do with union and this takes us on to his last problem.

That which is at the core of another person, what is inmost, the what-it-is-to-be this particular person cannot be communicated. I am I. You are you. I can never be you. Carson McCullers said that. A person is an incommunicable substance. Boethius said that. One person can never be annexed to another, fused with another.

So we have a central paradox. We want to be united, to be "oned" with what we love. We also feel that the best love is of what is special and central to another person. But the core of another person is exactly, exactly what one can never be united with because it incommunicable.

A choice between an impossibility (love without seeking union) and an illusion (love of what necessarily escapes us) -is this the Scylla and Charybdis of love? Or is there a way out? Before we look at Johann's response let's sum up. Three problems are in circulation: 1) Love is of the exterior only. 2) Direct love is not possible or too weak and dry. 3) If we can love the interior of another in the most profound love, what is loved is absolutely unattainable.

The solution to this problem, Johann claims, lies in the ancient metaphysical problem of the one and the many. [See our discussion: One Thread of Metaphysics]

What is the core of another person? -the incommunicable something, the "eye" of the "I"? The inmost, ownmost core of a person is his "act of existing". Unique, individual, incommunicable. Most hidden, most mysterious, most interior. Most real, most up-close. A person is a being who can utter "I am.". His interiority can be active and aware. Active and aware he can love himself.

He can also see, although never directly, that the other too is an "I" to himself. So by similitude and reflection he can love another as himself. But these are just starters, we do not yet have a foundation strong enough to support communion or community.

Here comes the metaphysics of the one and the many. Our own act of existence is not just mirrored in another. We are more than autonomous little diamonds that occur side by side. The act of existence of each person is from the same source–and that source is absolute, unbounded Subsistent Existence. Thus, in being open to and treasuring what appears most inaccessible (the inmost of another), I am, in fact, most in communion with myself, the other and the source.

Love at this level is defined by Johann as "active interiority and the adhesion of being to self." God or Subsistent Existence is self-giving. [In Christian theology, the Incarnation shows God as self-giving most intensely.]

A host of residual problems remain–fault, sin, false love, etc. How to love and love well or to endure the sufferings love brings - these are practical problems. But Johann thinks that with this framework the *theoretical problems* raised earlier vanish -in the sense that there is no metaphysical war between the self and the other, desire and benevolence, interiority and ecstasy.

Love is not corrupt because it is mixed with desire for one's own fullness. Johann says we are "called to fathom the value of self, to cherish it in its infinite Source, to commune with it in all its finite participations as it radiates from the faces of men."

"Thus man's destiny is ultimately not a pursuit but an unfolding. His goal is not a fragment on the horizon, but a God on whose fullness he draws." (p.79)

"Only by answering the gift of Self with the gift of himself can he ever fully and consciously be what he is. Only by animating the torrential multiplicity of his desires with the fire of a single love -a love whose term is ultimately more himself than he is himself -can he realize fully and consciously in his own life that interiority and adhesion to Being in which he participates, and that communion with Being to which he is called. Only by digging deep into the value of self will he break through to paradise." (p.80)

IX. A Question; A Thought Experiment; A Gathering

A question: Is it better to know or to love?

For Aquinas,[21] it is better to know things 'lower' than us and better to love things 'higher' than us. What is this? He assumes a hierarchy or pyramid of reality. Some things are realer than others. A photo is less real than its subject; a leaf is less real than a rabbit which is less real than a human. At the apex is the realest being, God.

He thinks of cognition or understanding as a kind of "taking in" and of love as a kind of "going out into". When we study botany we take into ourselves (in an immaterial way) the reality of a leaf etc. It is better to know a leaf because, in knowing, we bring the leaf up to our level. Falling in love with a leaf is unbelievable because you have to somehow get down to 'leaf level'. [Aquinas would add that a leaf exists in a higher mode in the mind of the botanist than in itself. Interesting or no, we would as lief leave leaves here.]

It is difficult to truly comprehend realities above us (and so to draw the greater into the lesser). But in loving something on a higher plane than I am, I am drawn into its superior reality and (in some way) rise up to share its excellence. We cannot engulf God with our concepts but in loving Him we can hope to be drawn into His reality and/or become more like Him.

What about realities on our own level? There is a certain equality among all human beings, at least in that they are human. For many, many reasons loving the other seems the better bet. A starter is that we don't seem to know ourselves very well. Let that suffice.

A thought experiment: What would a world be without love? Imagine a set of intellectual beings without any love whatever. They are aware of others, of a world around them, and they can reflect on this but it has no feel, no tone, no charge, no color to them.

Such beings have no interest in each other at all. They should not be caused. Since, reflecting on their dependence, they might be thankful which is a kind of affection, is it not? Leibniz' windowless monads at least mirror each other.

Biologists can find no such reality. Viruses might come close since they can continue for ages alone. And when they get active inside a cell, they show little concern for their hosts. But they do make copies of themselves and so act as if they were concerned about posterity.

Physics reports no such reality. Protons are attracted to electrons and repelled by other protons if the latter are outside their nuclear home. Electrons exchange photons. Quarks, feeling the 'color' of other quarks, communicate by gluons.[22]

Even the desire to dominate or the quest for glory involves connectedness with others. The residual question is why we connect in a twisted way.

Our thought experiment seems to collapse. We humans are 'highly connected' (to use a topological concept) with both the physical world and the intellectual world. We have more bacteria cells in our bodies than our own cells. We have more words of others 'in' our minds than words of our own coinage.

Why–what cause, what purpose?

A gathering: Josef Pieper finds the common thread in all love to be affirmation of existence.[23] "How good that you exist!" Seeing the goodness of one being opens the soul to realize "How wonderful that all this exists!"

Thus love is connected to happiness and can spread out to all existence. Many more questions could be raised. How do we know it is good to exist? or that I exist? or that you exist? If existence is good, what about problems like evil? For Pieper, this affirmation is metaphysically grounded through God in the relatedness of all existence. We flavor our closing with a few quotes.

> *Glücklich allein/Ist die Seele, die liebt.*
> Happy alone is the soul who loves.   –Goethe

> *Amor meus est pondus meus.*
> My love is my weight.   –Augustine

Fathers and teachers, I ponder 'What is hell?'
I maintain that it is the suffering of a being
unable to love. Once in infinite existence,
immeasurable in time and space, a spiritual
creature was given on his coming to earth,
the power of saying,"I am and I love"(ya yesm i ya lyublyu.)
–Father Zossima in Dostoevski's *Brothers Karamazov*

$$F=\frac{Gm_1m_2}{r^2}$$
                                            –Newton

> *l'amor che move il sole e altre stelle.*
> –Dante's ending to the Divine Comedy

X. Footnotes and References

1. Scholars cite Plato by the page and subdivisions of the Stephanus edition. *Symposium*, especially 198a-212c. See the *Phaedrus* for Plato's defense of love as divine madness. For the Theory of Forms see especially his *Republic*.
2. Aristotle, *Nicomachean Ethics*, Books viii and ix have most of the ideas on friendship. W.D. Ross is the main translator we have leaned upon.
3. The mother or benefactor paradox is from 1161b18-30 and 1167b16-1168a8. [Book viii ch 12 and ix ch7]

4. Hegel discusses the unhappy consciousness or alienated soul in the Phenomenology of Spirit, p.251. Caveat inceptor: (May the beginner beware): This is a tough book to solo through!

5. The teachings are to be found, of course, in the New Testament. See especially the Gospels of Luke and John, John's epistles and Paul's First Corinthians.

6. We use the term mystics for those who emphasize union with God. They have a lot to say about love. Works of many Jewish, Muslim, Christian, and Native Americans are available in *The Classics of Western Spirituality* (Paulist Press). Eastern mystics can best be tracked down through their respective traditions: Hindu, Zen etc.

7. Quotes from Sigmund Freud are all taken from *Group Psychology and Analysis of the Ego*, (tr. James Strachey) p.673 (Great Books edition). The theory permeates his work.

8. McCullers, Carson, *The Heart is a Lonely Hunter*, Bantam Books, New York, 1958. *The Member of the Wedding* and *The Ballad of the Sad Cafe* are also available in the *Collected Stories of Carson McCullers*, Houghton Mifflin, Boston, 1987. Pages given are from the Bantam Books editions.

9. In the *Ballad of the Sad Cafe* her characters are deformed. There she gives an explicit theory that the beloved is only a stimulus for the release of stored-up love. (p.18)

10. Heidegger, Martin, *Sein und Zeit (Being and Time)*, tr. John Macquarrie and Edward Robinson, Harper and Row, New York 1962). See p.31 English ed.

11. Boethius, *The Theological Tractates* (Loeb Classics, No. 74) p.85.

12. Solovyov, Vladimir, *The Meaning of Love*, (tr. Thomas R. Beyer, Jr., The Lindisfarne Press, West Stockbridge, MA, 1985).

13. Spinoza, Baruch, *Ethics*, (Book 4, proposition 44).

14. T.S. Eliot's *The Waste Land* shows the sort of fragmented consciousness that paralyzes love. He quotes F.H. Bradley's, *Appearance and Reality*: "My external perceptions are no less private to myself than are my thoughts or my feelings. In either case my experience falls within my own circle, a circle closed on the outside; and, with all its elements alike, every sphere is opaque to the others which surround it." (p.306 of Bradley's work). For an undermining of love based on will see Thomas Hobbes, *Leviathan*.

15. Swinburne, Algernon, lines 35-36 from *Poems and Ballads.*

16. Nygren, Andres, *Agape and Eros* (tr. Philip Watson, Westminister Press) is a Christian rejection of eros.

17. Heidegger, *Being and Time*, p.98

18. Kitaro, Nishida, *Zen no kenkyu* (A Study of Good, tr. V.H. Viglielmo, Tokyo, 1960). Cited from the Encyclopedia of Philosophy, vol. 5, p. 519.

19. Ratzinger, Joseph, *Eschatology: Death and Eternal Life*, tr. Michael Waldstein, CUA Press 1988, p.155.

20. Johann, Robert, *The Meaning of Love*, Paulist Press, Glen Rock, NJ, 1966.

21. Aquinas, *Summa Theologica*, I, q82 a3. See also Part I-II q65a5 where charity is called a certain mutual love and communication. See also II-II q23 to q27.

22. Physical theories change quickly. (QCD) Quantum chromodynamics studies quarks, gluons, etc. An introductory discussion is Chris Quigg, *Scientific American*, April 1985, p.84.

23. Pieper, Josef, *Über die Liebe, (About Love)*, tr. Richard and Clara Winston, Franciscan Herald Press, Chicago, 1974).

—The index on love in *The Great Books of the Western World*, vol. 2, p.1058-1082 is a good place to chase down Lucretius, Dante, Pascal, etc. *Philosophies of Love*, David Norton and Mary Kille, Rowman and Allanheld, 1983 arranges articles around six types of love. We stress rather the unity of love.

XI. Questions

I

1) Several questions were raised on at the beginning of this chapter. Take two of these and give the answer of a) one theory from this chapter, b) an outside source.

2) Is brotherly/sisterly love a special kind? If so, what is special about it?

3) Christianity affirms friendship with God. Find and explicate another tradition that also does.

4) How does friendship differ from loyalty or alliance?

5) How is love related to: sympathy, empathy, hatred, indifference, pity, admiration, wonder?

6) Love seems to be both a feeling and an act of the will. Develop/compare/contrast these two senses.

7) Why is there so much hurt with love -even mystics tell of it in their search for God.

II

1) What is Kant's or Hegel's notion of love?

2) Comment on some of Augustine's ideas on love.

3) Choose an atheistic philosopher (Sartre, Hobbes, etc.) and explain his notion of love.

4) Draw out a theory of love from a major writer (Chaucer, Cervantes, Goethe, etc.) or a major work (Romeo and Juliet, Crime and Punishment, etc.).

5) Compare Plato's idea to that of a)Jesus' b)Freud or c)McCullers. Develop or challenge one comparison.

6) What philosophical notions are destructive of love. For example, if one says that truth is relative, how does this bear on love? Give any thinker's view.

7) What is Lucretius' notion of love? How might this compare to Freud's?

III

1)What is the connection between a)love and happiness, b)love and free will, c)love and immortality? For example, to what extent can/can't you control who/what you are fond of?

2) Aristotle has three kinds of friendship. If you think there is another kind, elaborate on it.

3) What is the connection between our ability/inability to know another and ability/inability to love another?

4) What does the fact of love prove or indicate about human nature or reality in general?

5) McCullers connects love and time. Develop or challenge that view.

6) In what sense can animals be said to love? In what way are they suitable objects of love?

7) If there are beings (other than God) higher than humans, how are they to love and be loved by us?

EXISTENCE OF GOD

Introduction

Atheism
1. Infinites
2. Suffering
3. Fault
4. Ugliness/Stupidity
5. Ockham's Razor
6. Stupidity of Natural Laws
7. Excludes Freedom
8. Feeling of Absence
9. Childish Notion
10. Anti-Ontological

Theism

CAUSE
1. Self Existing Being
2. First Mover
3. First Cause
4. Directing Mind
5. Cause of Infinite Desire
6. Cause of Infinite Idea
7. Necessary Being
8. Particularity of the Universe

PERFECTION, BEAUTY, GOODNESS
9. Degrees of Reality
10. Beauty

PURPOSE, GOAL, GROUND
11. Ground of Morality/Giver of Justice
12. Willingness to Die
13. Ground of Science/Truth
14. Meaning
15. Sufficient Reason

Footnotes/References

Introduction

Since it is impossible to prove opposites, it is not a matter of giving equal time to both sides. Nor are there only two sides. There are ideas that something "trans" exists but "it" is so far from any common notion of God that we don't include such here -the idea of the perfectibility of the human race, an end point of evolution, the oceanic feeling, etc.

And there is agnosticism -which comes in many flavors: God may exist but: I don't know; nobody knows; it has not been shown so far; it cannot be known or shown; it can be shown that it cannot be shown;[1] it is of no interest; etc.

Finally there is a faith that draws on revelation. Philosophy is limited to human reason. But if philosophy can also show God's existence, it doesn't compete with faith nor claim to have a better "handle" on God than faith does. Quite the opposite, philosophical theism would open a road to those who have no other access. [Of course, if atheism were demonstrable, then philosophy would quarrel with faith.] Faith grasps what is beyond reason not what is against it.

To show God's existence we really need two steps: 1)to show something special exists and 2)to show this is God. We obviously cannot demonstrate everything about God. Did He reveal Himself to Moses or Muhammed? Philosophy cannot decide. The Christian mysteries of the Incarnation and the Trinity cannot be demonstrated.

Do we need a definition of God before setting out? A problem. Theists don't claim that we can define God the way we can define a rhombus–saying exactly what it is. This would mean we could circle

God in our comprehension, put Him under our microscope–and then He wouldn't be God. They use words that point to, rather than define, God. Supreme Being, First Cause, Highest Being are such. More powerful notions are Anselm's "that than which nothing greater can be thought" and Aquinas' esse subsistens, the subsisting to be. Philosophical theists (we prefer this to "believers" for those who hold that the existence of God is demonstrable) are quite content to show that something special exists and that it is like God–in that it has some of the chief attributes of God. Then there can't be two realities, what-was-shown and God. What-was-shown is God as far as philosophy can manifest Him.

Several of these arguments claim to do at least that. Others are much weaker, they are 'evidences' only. Atheists counter notions of the divine by raising objections and difficulties. Few claim an iron-clad proof that there can be no God. Again, we present both strong arguments and mere evidences.

Please keep in mind the logic of all this. If even one argument "works", the others can be let alone. But opposing arguments should be neutralized. What if one remains unconvinced by all arguments? The believer is left where he was before -proof is not necessary. So is the unbeliever. But let's not idle (idol) here. Enormous thought lies in front of us. We have tried to arrange the arguments logically, not chronologically nor by their usual historical names.

ATHEISM

1. Infinites

If God were infinite goodness or an infinitely good reality, then the good would fill up everything. All would be "full up" with goodness. There would be no room for evil. There would be no evil. However, there are evils. So there is no God.[2]

2. Suffering

Evils have been classified as of two kinds: the evil of suffering or pain, 'physical evil' or poena, and the evil of fault or guilt, moral evil or culpa. Culpa is rooted in the free choice of some agent. Poena is not. The two may occur together, of course. If someone shoots himself in the foot to avoid being sent on a worthy but dangerous mission, the pain in his foot and his loss of mobility is poena, but the cowardly action and loss of nobility is culpa.

If God is all-good and all-powerful he should have made a world without suffering or poena. Therefore: i) God is not all-good or ii)God is not all-powerful or iii)God is neither.

This is a trilemma. We are hooked on one of these three horns: God either can grant your prayer but doesn't want to or wants to but can't or neither wants to nor can. Since the notion of God includes both omnipotence and benevolence, this argument is also used to reject God's existence.

3. Fault

Some add that God could and should prevent moral evil as well. God could make man so that he would be free and yet would always choose the good.

This[3,4] is made in response to Augustine who argues that evil does not disprove God, saying: Suffering was originally caused by moral evil. Moral evil in turn is rooted in the creature's freedom. If man is given freedom to love the good or not, then it must be possible that someone, sometime not love the good. [That someone *actually* fail morally is an empirical fact, though not a necessity.] Evils exist then, only because God allows them in choosing a greater good for the creature. To love freely is a greater good than to love unfreely.

Augustine adds that evil is a lack, a species of non- being. For him, these notions counter all three arguments.

4. Ugliness/Stupidity

Just as some are entranced by the beauty and order in things, others are stunned by the ugliness, stupidity, waste and disorder all around them. In the 20th century over one hundred million people have been killed by others. Fish lay zillions of eggs but only a handful survive. The earth may be a beautiful blue home, but the other eight planets are too hot, too cold or too full of poisonous gases. Ticks, mosquitoes, and viruses seem eternal, the butterfly may die in few days. Much of life is so ordinary–a myrmecoid (antlike) continuation of custom interrupted by mindless change. Why is beauty rare, if God is beautiful?

5. Ockham's Razor

Physics, biology and chemistry advance from success to success. The formulas of molecules, the motions of planets and rivers, the structure of cells, chromosomes, brain, eye, atomic nucleus, etc. are understood in more detail year by year. From quasar to quark, scientists go from explanation to explanation like a salesman from door to door. Nowhere in the "salesman's pitch" is an appeal to God.

Ockham's razor is the principle that we should use only as few explanatory factors as are required to explain something. [Called a principle of logic–Ockham's principle is not a logical requirement at all. Even if one motive were enough to explain a murder, the killer may have had several.]

So God should be left out.

[A counter is made that science talks of the how, of change and of 'essences' within nature. It does not reach to the 'whether', to existence, to why things are as they are, to why there is a world at all.]

6. Stupidity of Natural Laws

While it takes a good intelligence to understand the laws of science, the laws themselves reveal how stupid the world is, if we look at them in a certain way:[5]

Physics: The law of inertia says that things do nothing unless they are pushed and then they keep on doing what they were pushed to do. The conservation laws tell us the things that remain the same are odd things like isospin or angular momentum, while what we love is scattered and shattered, torn away and worn away. The quantum theory says we can't even tell that much. Microevents are in principle haphazard.

Chemistry: Entropy says that things are getting more random and disorderly all the time. Other explanations are made by the principle of least energy or laziness.

So nature starts out randomly and then gets more and more slovenly unless its own laziness gets in the way.

Biology: Fitness doesn't mean being tuned to the deep harmonics of nature, it means surviving a death threat. 'Natural selection' is negative–those who don't fit die. In genetics (where we do think of positive causes) like produces like by a kind of blind auto-xeroxing (independent assortment of alleles), except when like produces unlike by random mutations which are capricous and nearly all fatal.

Newer sciences like sociobiology move to explain our favorite flavors, costumes and customs by the same types of causes. They follow an ancient path. Lucretius[6], e.g., seats human consciousness and love in the pings and pangs of mental molecules. Hobbes[7] extends this notion to politics.

Can there be an Intelligent Designer behind all this?

7. Excludes Freedom

Is freedom incompatible with God's causality and foreknowledge? [See our Freedom]

Here Sartre[8] makes a different argument: Man's existence or that-man-is is simply there. But man's essence or what- man-is is up to his own free making. The project of man is to make himself, to forge his own essence, to turn his potentiality into actuality. If there be any human nature or blueprint, intelligible from the start, then the project of man would still be to turn his potentiality into actuality, but the potentiality would be mapped out beforehand. Human freedom would be confined to choosing to fulfill his nature or not. Man would not have the radical freedom to construct who he is.

If there were a creator, presumably he would create according to some idea or plan. Man's freedom would be hostage to that plan. So there is no God. His notion of human self-creation gives to humans more than theists claim for God. Is it a description, dream or nightmare? For Sartre, "authentic" man faces down the nausea {etymologically `sea- sickness'} that comes with realizing we are forever at sea–as he charts a course without map, compass, stars, bailer, haven or shore.

8. Feeling of Absence

You walk down a street littered with garbage. You stub your toe. Trivialities or tragedies -where's God? Theologians may expostulate on the ineffability, transcendence, and immanence of God -but still we are (often, at least) left with the feeling of being empty of God. God seems even more absent, perhaps, in the case of trivialities.

Even those most drenched with a sense of God report the same feeling. Once when Teresa of Avila[9] stepped in a puddle she is said to have said: If this is how you treat your friends no wonder you have so few!

If even those who do pray can experience such emptiness, how can nonbelievers be persuaded that God is.

9. Childish Notion

Freud's *The Future of an Illusion* is about religion[10]. He said, "This consists in its religious ideas in the widest sense–in other words (which will be justified later) in its illusions." His argument is basically that it is childish to believe in God. Belief in God is part of the childhood of individuals, and of the childhood of our species (primitives) and of those who have never really emerged from childhood (neurotics). Freud thought the study of primitives would give us a window into neurotics because both were frozen in the mindscape of children. When man and mankind grew up, religion would vaporize.

[Why include such arrogance and ignorance? Primitives are not children. Nor does calling something childish prove a lot. Going to the moon was a childish notion once. But we include this as representative of those who do think the notion of God is unenlightened.]

I call this the 'Santa Claus argument'. As we grow up we don't develop a sophisticated 'clausology' to explain Santa's non-presence (or is it his non-presents!). We just set the whole thing aside when we realize how the world works.

[But we reject the Claus not the cause! We set Santa aside when we find the true cause of the presents!]

10. Anti-Ontological

Why would a Perfect Being create at all? Full, happy, he need not concern himself with creating a world. What reason could he have? Is God whimsical? capricious? Yet the world exists.

Since this takes the notion of God and folds it over to deny such a being -I call it an anti-ontological argument.

To rephrase: If a Perfect Being exists, it cannot have any 'foreign affairs' or activities outside itself. Then all that is would be God'and would be within the self-luminous fountain of conscious, joyful perfection. This is not so. {Sankara[11] says it is so.} Therefore no such being exists.

[But does generosity have to imply a lack? Is calling a friend to share a piece of good news a shortcoming?]

THEISM

1. Self-Existing Being

A) A short version:

Nothingness has no power to produce any being at all nor to produce one kind of being rather than another. So whatever comes to be requires another being to draw it into existence. At least one dependent being exists (me, for example). If every being were derived from some other being, we would have an infinite series of dependent beings. But such a series is itself dependent. So unless we are prepared to go back and credit nothingness as a cause, there must be (at least one) non-dependent or self-existing being. Such does not come into existence, it simply is.

[Other 'properties' that follow on the idea of self-existence are discussed in the longer version below.]

B) Fuller version:

    i) Some things exist.

    ii) Nothingness, non-being has no power to produce anything at all nor any kind of thing in particular.

    iii) Therefore, any being whatever has its existence either from another or from itself.

iv) It is not possible that every being exist by another (have a derived, dependent being).

Let us examine three cases: a)circular b)non-circular finite c)non-circular infinite.

In case a, we have a scenario like this: A causes B. B causes C. C causes D. D causes A. Here A is both a cause of D (through intermediates B and C) and is caused by D. So A exists before it exists! Contradiction.

In case b, we start with a present reality X_n and go back through a finite set of intermediates until we reach X_1. Since X_1 is the first in the series, it is not derived from any other. So it is a self-existing being.

In case c, we start with any dependent or caused being (called E for effect). The cause of this being is itself also caused and so it too is an effect. This continues 'backwards' without end. Since all are effects and there is no way of numbering them, we write the series simply as

$$... \longrightarrow E \longrightarrow E \longrightarrow E \longrightarrow E \text{ (any present effect)}$$

Some say such a series is impossible. If so, the case is proven. But let's suspend this issue and imagine that we can think this series. The claim is now made that such a series itself is dependent, infinite or no. The length of a queue doesn't explain why there is a queue. If any element of the series demands a cause (and this is granted), how can adding more such elements satisfy the demand (no matter how many more are added)?

No matter how the argument is delayed or prolonged the conclusion is forced upon us (unless we allow nothingness to produce things, which has been rejected) that:

v) There is at least one self-existing being (SEB). Let's explore what else can be deduced from this idea.

vi) The SEB is unlimited. It cannot be limited from without because it is not dependent on others, it exists of itself. It cannot be limited from within because limitation is something imposed. What does this mean? If you ask why a wall is painted only so red (say pink) and not redder, I cannot answer because of the red but because of the white paint that was added. If you ask why a lion is only so strong and not stronger, I must mention something other than his strength. Otherwise I am blaming strength for lack of strength, saying red is the cause of unred. We apply this 'metaphysical' notion (the limitedness of x is always due to something other than x) to an SEB. An SEB cannot be limited from within or without. Therefore, an SEB is unlimited.

[Another argument might be made based on simplicity. A composite has parts. If the parts are in some way prior to the whole, then the composite must be put together. Then it must have an origin or cause, it cannot be an SEB. Thus the SEB is simple. Might this eliminate some SEB contenders?]

vii) There is only one SEB. For two things to be different, they must differ in some way or else they would coalesce into one. If there were two SEB's one would have to have something the other lacked. But the SEB as unlimited cannot lack or be incomplete.

viii) The SEB is eternal. As self-existing the SEB cannot be brought into existence; nor can it be separated from its existence (and perish thereby) since its existence is through itself.

ix) The SEB can be called God. Our notion of God overflows what is said here, but there cannot be both God and the SEB distinct from God. Since there is exactly one SEB, then the SEB is God.

2. First Mover or Unchanged Changer (Prime Mover)

Thomas Aquinas advances five ways to show God exists.[12] "I say the existence of God can be proven in five ways. The first and more manifest way is taken from motion. For it is certain from the senses that some things are moved in this world. However, everything that is moved, is moved by another. For nothing is moved unless it is in potency to that toward which it is moved: but something moves in as much as it is in act. For to move is nothing other than to draw something from potency to act: however something cannot be brought from potency to act, except by some being in act: thus fire, which is actually hot, makes wood which is potentially hot, to be actually hot, and through this changes and alters it.

Moreover, it is not possible that a thing be in act and potency with respect to the same thing at the same time, but only with respect to different things. For what is hot in act cannot simultaneously be cold in act, but is cold in potency. Therefore it is impossible that a thing be both mover and moved in the same respect and at the same time, or that it move itself. Thus, everything that is moved must be moved by another. So if that by which a thing is moved, is itself moved, it must be moved by another, and that by another.

However this cannot proceed to infinity, because then there would not be a first mover; and consequently no other movers, because the subsequent movers do not move unless they are put in motion by the first mover, as the stick is not moved unless it is moved by the hand. So it is necessary to come to some first mover, which is moved by nothing: and this all understand to be God."

Aquinas calls this "the more manifest way" -but it needs a few clarifications. For one thing, today `mover' can mean `one who is moving' but to Thomas it means `one who causes motion or change' and this must be in another not in oneself. Also, today motion usually means `locomotion', but for Thomas it means `change' including such things as blushing or getting tired.

To some the Law of Inertia means that if a body is moving now, that is enough to explain its motion yesterday and back through an infinite number of yesterdays. So it is not necessary to have a first. Newton[13] said once something has a certain amount of motion, forces are required only to change the motion, but the whole system proceeds from God.

Still, to sidestep quarrels over physics and to be more in step with Aquinas here, we render motion as change and so the First Mover is the Unchanged Changer.

To restate the argument:

1)Some things change. 2)Nothing can change itself. Whatever is changed is changed by another. 3)A series of changed changers must have a first or else there will be no subsequent changers. 4)So, there exists an unchanged changer.

Might there be more than one, e.g., one for every chain of changes? We leave this for another day. Who is troubled at the prospect of many Gods? The first premise is evident. The logic seems valid. The argument hangs on Premises #2 and #3.

Premise #2. Change is understood as something's going from being potentially x to being actually x. For example, an apple rip-

Existence of God

ens -it goes from being potentially red to actually red. Growth and ripening are not things an apple does to itself. Sun and soil help make its sugars. Nothing can change itself because that would involve giving itself something (redness) that it doesn't have (because it is green). For Thomas the controlling principle is: *Nihil dat quod non habet.* Nothing can give what it does not have. The sun does not have chlorophyll, nor does it give it. But the causes in toto have the reality or power to do what they do.

Premise #3. Change sets up a series. Let's go back along the series. Changes in the apple are brought about by chemical reactions in the apple and in the leaves, and these by changes in the strength and length of the sunlight. These, in turn, are changed by the position of the earth changing and this by the earth's tilt and velocity and these by the sun's gravity and this by the sun's mass etc., etc., etc.

Aquinas rejects a "firstless" series or one which would 'procede to infinity' here and elsewhere. Let us look at two reasons for rejecting any infinite series explanation.

i) even if there were an infinite series it would not explain what is needed.

ii) certain kinds of infinite series are excluded.

Case i) was already considered in the argument (for a self-existing being) that even an infinite series of dependent beings remains dependent. This type of argument might also be developed here and in the next argument for an Uncaused Cause.

Case ii) involves a series of "essentially ordered" elements or causes or 'changers'. Essentially ordered changers are changers that are needed here and now to bring about change here and now.

Suppose I wish to paint. The brush, paint, canvas, my arm, hand and attention, etc. are needed here and now to paint here and now. These are essentially ordered. The hand must function to move the brush. The brush must function to move the paint.

Not all series of changers or causes are essentially ordered. I must have parents, grandparents, great-grandparents, etc. to paint since I need them to exist. But they don't have to act or exist here and now for me to paint here and now. They are not essentially ordered causes.

To return to essentially ordered causes -if an infinite series of brushes, paints, canvas, easel, atmospheric conditions, terrestrial conditions, solar conditions, etc., must be summoned up and set to work to produce a painting, you can be sure no painting will come forth. So if you see someone painting you can be sure it depends on only a finite set of essential changers. Start with the paint going on the canvas (the 'last one') and go back through brush, hand, etc. Without specifying each supporting element, we know that if the series is finite, it has a first.

This first changer is not changed by another since it is first and it is not changed by itself since nothing changes itself. So it is completely unchanged or immutable.

[How about spontaneous changes–a man falls through a trap door, a chemical reaction occurs spontaneously, a nucleus emits a beta particle?

If these events just pop up and are truly causeless, then arguments from causality and change go by the board -not only in philosophical theology but in natural science as well. Included in this wholesale dismissal would be the very arguments to show the existence of the beta particle in the first place. Strange and strained.

A more relaxed explanation seems to be that either productive causes of events like beta-decay can be found or these events involve the removal or collapse or loss or defect in required supporting causes.

A roofer climbs to a high rung on a wooden ladder. He puts work, energy, 'cause', into his elevated position. Now he 'should' fall but is constrained by the strength of the wood, skill of the carpenter, etc. He falls if the step breaks, not spontaneously, but because the cause he needs to stay up is removed and gravity takes over.

To force an explanation of beta-decay would be weak. But if we allow even one holiday from causality we have to allow for any number, undermining all causal reasoning.]

3. First Efficient Cause or Uncaused Cause

Thomas says: "The second way is from efficient causality. For we find in sensible things an order of efficient causes; we do not find, nor is it possible that a thing be the efficient cause of itself;

because then it would be prior to itself which is impossible. Moreover it is not possible to proceed to infinity in efficient causes. Because in all ordered efficient causes, the first is the cause of the intermediate and the intermediate is the cause of the last, whether the intermediate are many or one. If the cause is removed, the effect is removed. Therefore, if there were not a first efficient cause, there would not be an intermediate or a last. But if one may proceed to infinity in efficient causes, there would not be a first efficient cause, and so there would not be a last effect, nor intermediate causes which is obviously false. Therefore, it is necessary to posit some first efficient cause: which all call God."

1) Some things come to be and are caused by others.
2) Nothing can bring itself into existence.
3) A series of caused causes must have a first or else there would be no subsequent causes.
4) Therefore, there exists an uncaused cause.

#1 is obvious. At least one dependent being is needed -take yourself! #2 is discussed above. #3 is the pivotal claim. We discussed it at length in the Prime Mover argument. This argument parallels the Prime Mover argument. But all details and theories of change disappear. It focuses on existence and its conclusion is stronger–not merely immutable but uncaused being.

4. Directing Mind/Intelligence behind Nature and Instinct

This is commonly called a teleological argument -one based on nature as being purposeful or having a final cause. As such it runs into difficulties (and ridicule) from some theories of evolution. Such criticism may aim more directly at those for whom nature has its own purposes.

Thomas[14] says: "The fifth way is taken from the governance of things. For we see that some things that lack knowledge, namely natural bodies, act for a purpose: this is evident from the fact that they always or frequently act in the same way, to attain that which is best; whence it is evident that they attain to the end not by chance but by intention. However, those things that do not have knowledge do not tend to an end unless directed by something which is knowing and understanding, as the arrow is directed by the archer. Therefore, there is some intelligence by which all natural things are directed to an end."

1) To act according to a complex plan requires intelligence.
2) Yet some animals etc., so act but lack intelligence.
3) Therefore, they are directed by an intelligence outside themselves or outside nature.

Let us look at the premises together. Some animals act in a very complex way. Frisch[15] has studied honey bees. How do they tell the others back home where the good flowers are? They do a dance–a logarithmic dance where the ratio of wiggles to waggles tells the distance and the angle to the sun, etc. Or somesuch.

What is this language of rythms and logarithms? Does the honeybee know math? Does it have within a conscious pattern by which it acts? Is it like a builder who follows a design in his own mind? Or one who only can read a blueprint but not visualize the overall structure? Or one who can follow direct instruction but not a blueprint? Or is it a speaker (dancer) of language who correctly uses a grammar he does not understand?

The inner world of animals is a closed book, but we see only these possibilities for our little honey bee:

i) it actually does think it out or at least has learned it as we learn a language.

ii) it acts according to a plan that it is unconscious of, but that is programmed into it -isn't this what we mean by instinct?

iii) it acts by chance

iv) there is neither inner thought nor inner program - then it must be directed from without, if chance is rejected.

Aquinas assumes i) is out as a matter of common sense and iii) is out for complex processes at least. This leaves only an external director or an internal program. If one opts for an internal program, won't it be fair to ask about the program's cause, about the Programmer?

The rejection of chance is of current interest again because of the René Thom's[16] catastrophe theory and various chaos theories.

Aquinas might argue as so many have since his time: If a cat let loose on a computer were to type 'type' we should not immediately believe it a miracle. With 103 keys the odds are 1:112,550,880. But we may think it just happened. Also t and y are close together, so the realistic odds may be much less. And many other combinations are words. But if it typed "Frisch weht der Wind/ Der Heimat zu/ Mein Irisch Kind,/ Wo weilest du?",[17] it would take a rabid ailurophile not to believe there was some outside assistance being given. And if the cat typed *As You Like It* in respectible idiomatic Chuvash–well, if you can believe that sort of thing happens by chance, then the 'fifth way' is not for you!

[It is said that evolutionary theory[18] destroys this argument. According to this idea the 'fit' and hence the pattern and purpose we see in nature is actually the result of natural selection. If white bears are found in snowy regions and dark bears in wooded ones, this is not due to any cunning in nature but to the blind fact that if the bears had other colors they would long since have been eliminated. But this way does not claim that nature itself is intelligently purposeful. It is about the cause of complex, intelligent-seeming action in unintelligent beings. As such might it be 'evolution-friendly'? Darwin himself was amazed at the complexity of the human ear and eye.]

One side-argument here is about the cause of order in nature. If nature is an ordered thing, and if it lacks the means for this order within it–then can't we point to the Great Orderer without?

In Newton's day a brilliant mathematics seemed to tell of a world of clocklike precision. Today quantum mechanics, fractal geometry, statistical thermodynamics, chaos theory, evolution etc., challenge how we can think of nature as ordered or even what order means.

The popularity (if not the truth) of arguments from order rise and fall with scientific models. We leave it as a question: If nature can be understood by an intellect that didn't create it (human scientist) and if nature itself does not possess intellect–does it have to be made or guided by another intelligence?

5. Cause of Infinite Desire

No matter how much we have, we want more and more. Pascal says we are always about to be happy but never are. But why is this? Strictly two issues are raised–the cause and the goal of endless yearning.

What is its cause? Is it just because we can see something else down the road? That doesn't seem to account for it because we apprehend many things without hankering after them. Is infinite longing a spin-off of another part of human nature or it is an ingredient in itself? A finite cause of something infinite does not seem possible. The only possible source then is infinite–God.

Is the goal real? God or a Fata Morgana?

If there is a real goal, it cannot be any finite good since then we will want more than what such a good can fulfill. The striving itself is taken for a fact. If there is no infinite goal, then the striving itself is absurd or at least necessarily frustrated. If we view the striving as absurd then we have come to reason that life is unreasonable. Is reasoning to the unreasonable itself unreasonable?

The other choice is that there actually is an infinite good toward which we strive–God.

6. Cause of Infinite Idea

Rene Descartes[19] claims he has an idea of God, i.e., a substance that is infinite, eternal, immutable, independent, all-knowing, all-powerful, etc. Where does it come from?

The word 'idea' can be used ambiguously to mean psychological event; general concept (regardless of its being thought by anyone at the moment); the actual object thought of; the pure essence or form of a thing; etc. He seems to mean 'a content of mind actually being thought now'. These have three sources: i) they come from without, e.g. the ringing of a bell, ii) they are rooted in the understanding, e.g. theorems of mathematics, iii) they are formed by the imagination, e.g. a winged horse. In Meditations III and Discourse on Method IV he argues that this notion has been placed in him by God.

To discuss this further we need to take on epistemology (a subject we put off to later philosophy) and much of the entire Cartesian system. Further, scholars claim Descartes often deliberately argues in a sense opposite to his actual aim.

Here let us ponder: What kind of causes do thoughts have? How is it that we have notions like pure justice, pure truth etc.? Do we get notions of perfections simply by cancelling flaws and faults in the observable world or in ourselves? Does the thought of God need a special cause?

7. Necessary Being

In logic, necessity applies to propositions rather than to individual beings. So we can say "A bachelor is an unmarried man." is necessary without saying that bachelors are necessary beings.

Those who apply the term to individual beings may do so in two ways: i) necessary beings are permanent, not subject to rust, rot, ruin. For some ancients, stars were such beings. Modern science may deny any such or it may look upon the proton, quark or gluon (or perhaps momentum or mass-energy) in this way -the verdict is not in. ii) necessary means 'has to be', 'has its existence built in'.

Contingent can be the opposite for either sense.

Al-Farabi[20] says, "Contingent beings have had a beginning. Now that which begins to exist must owe its existence to the action of a cause. This cause, in turn, either is or is not contingent. If it is contingent, it also must have received its existence by the action of another cause, and so on. But a series of contingent beings which would produce one another cannot proceed to infinity or move in a circle. Therefore, the series of causes and effects must arrive at a cause that holds its existence from itself and this is the first cause."

Avicenna[21] says, "...being is either contingent or necessary. If it is necessary then the point we sought to prove is established. If on the other hand it is contingent, that which is contingent cannot enter upon being except for some reason which sways the scales in favor of its being and against its non-being. If the reason is also contingent, then there is a chain of contingents linked one to the other, and there is no being at all; for this being which is the subject of our hypothesis cannot enter into being so long as it is not preceded by an infinite succession of beings, which is absurd. Thus contingent beings end in a necessary being."

Aquinas[22] says, "However every necessary thing either has the cause of its necessity from another or not. It is not possible to proceed to infinity in necessary beings which have a cause of their necessity, as neither in efficient causes as has been proven. Therefore we must posit something which is per se necessary, not having the cause of its necessity from another, but which is the cause of the necessity of others: which all call God."

The core idea of all these: Even if things like protons are permanent beings, there must be (at least) one being which is not merely permanent but that has its existence in and of itself. So this is like the self-existing argument.

8. Particularity of the Universe -The Great Exnihilator

Mortimer Adler[23] argues to God not from the existence but from the particularity of the universe: Annihilation means to reduce a thing to nothingness, not merely to destroy it. 'Exnihilation' is his coin for the exact opposite -giving some thing to be from no previous material. The argument: 1) This world could be otherwise than it is. 2) So it is merely a possible cosmos, not a necessary one. (What is necessary cannot be other than it is.) 3) So it is capable of not being. 4) What is merely capable of being needs a cause of coming to be, of being the way it is and of remaining in being (lest it slip into nothingness). 5) Therefore, there exists right now–the Great Exnihilator.

For Adler the key premise is #1. Those who deny it have to say that each little thing, e.g., the color of the clothes you are wearing right now -cannot be otherwise. Nature cannot be the cause since science shows natural causes to involve only change -whether in chemistry (conservation of energy) or biology (evolution not origination).

[But is he confusing two senses of possible: i) could be otherwise and ii) could not be at all? If I throw dice on the floor, 8 is a possible score but there must be some score.]

9. Degrees of Reality

Thomas Aquinas[24] says, "The fourth way is taken from the gradations which are found in things. For some things are more and less good, true, noble and so of other qualities of this kind. But more and less are said of diverse things according to how they approach in different ways to something which is maximum, as the hotter is that which approaches more to the hottest. Therefore there is something which is most true, most good and most noble, and consequently most in being [maxime ens]: ... "

1) Some things are truer, nobler, "gooder", "realer". [A man is more real than his photograph.]

2) It is impossible to have degrees unless they are being compared to a standard -even if the standard is not a readily accessible physical thing. One photograph is better than another because it is a closer likeness to the real man. Blood is redder than brick -you have an idea of redness to compare them to. No better without a best.

3) There exists a "realest" being (maxime ens).

The first premise is for most of us common sense. Yet there are those who think it would be 'anthropocentric' to say that a panda is more real than a parsnip and 'judgmental' to say that Beethoven is more musical than a heavy metal group. They claim all preferences are simply a matter of subjective evaluations and no one else has a right to impose his on others. Although some claim this moral and ontological relativism in theory, who carries it out in practice? For example, if a man rescued an old album rather than a child from a fire–who would say that was OK, just a matter of one's subjective viewpoint?

The argument hangs on the notion that there are degrees not just in quality and quantity but in 'being'–that some entities are more real than others.

The second premise is the unusual one. Can you say 2+2=5 is getting closer than 2+2=100 unless there is a true answer to this sum. You can't get nearer to Paris unless it exists. Thomas adds that the maximum in a genus is the cause of all in that genus. This is another claim. Even if true, do we need it if the `maximum being' is already identifiable as God?

An intermission is called for: To philosophical theists some of the above arguments are absolutely certain–apodictic. Then why add others that are "weaker"? Is this a concession of failure? No. An argument may be stronger in itself, but not for some people. Metaphysics is not to everyone's taste. Some deny it any validity, some can't understand it, some find it too abstract and cold. If God exists, is there any harm in arriving at this conclusion by different roads?
----

10. Beauty

A beautiful sunset, a distant bell, a pretty face -and we are drawn out of ourselves. We feel pulled to something. Maybe it's just the face or the bell. Maybe. Or is there something more? A hint at hidden depths? An evocation of distant mystery? A distant mystery suddenly brought up close?

Or is it just the two of us there in the sunset: The fragile reed which is my strip of space-time and the scarlet sinking sphere?

Intimations are not proofs. But we ask of such experience, not just its cause or purpose but what exactly is it an experience of? For Plato, beautiful realities (beautifuls) participate in Beauty Itself.[25] Any experience of beauty sets us on the trail to Beauty. He doesn't say Beauty Itself is God, but he calls one who loves Beauty theophilei–a friend/lover of God.

A thought lands softly on the "hidden excitement", awestruck, "drawn out of oneself". If our sense of depth in beauty is not an illusion, if there is a reality of which we merely pick up traces, won't it be sublimely beautiful?

11. Ground of Morality/Giver of Justice

Immanuel Kant[26] argues: We should act out of duty which means to do what is right, even if this is against our own inclination or profit. But so acting doesn't automatically make us satisfied and happy. It may even bring suffering and death. Acting out of duty makes us worthy of happiness.

So what? Does being worthy have any payoff? If so, we envision something like God to grant the worthy gladness.

The alternative is simply that there is no justice. This is more than a wish unfulfilled–it is a very aggressive kind of distortion because: We have reason which tells us how we should act. At the same time, this kind of action doesn't lead to what we know we wish–happiness. So then reason is a compass that keeps taking us off course, a detector that conceals the very treasure we use the detector for. We are then programmed to fail! The program (reason) that allows us to see and anticipate results of action is, at the same time, what precludes fruition–because duty does not bring fruition here and there is no there.

Now, if there is a God such a program might make sense.The purpose of the program is not for engulfing happiness here but for lining ourselves up with something beyond. Otherwise, not just us, but the whole universe itself is a "moral black hole" that sucks in all good deeds and karma credit cards and returns nothing. As if there were a cosmic comic with a bad sense of humor!

12. Willingness to Die

Many people are willing to give up their lives for something–for a child, for friends, for country, for ideals like justice or truth. Some are atheists. We ask what underlies this willingness, what protects it from absurdity. To begin with, one's own continued biological life cannot be the greatest thing in existence. If it were, then trading it in for something else would be absurd indeed. [Could this point be used to build a psychological argument for the immortality of the person?]

Then we look for something larger and actually more loved by a person than his own (biological) self.

a)Perhaps it is another person. Romeo and Juliet are willing to die, not even to preserve the other's life, but in sorrow at the loss of the other.

However does this escape absurdity? Aren't human selves, in a sense, on the same level of reality? [Would you give your life to save that of a Nobel Prize winner simply because the other is a Nobel Prize winner?] To give your life for a pet or a parking space is irrational because these are on lower levels of reality than you are. To give your life for your friend may involve more than an exchange of one life for another. If only such an exchange is involved, problems remain. For one thing, you would wish the best to your friend and that best would include that he be a generous hero. Generous enough to give his life for his friend. So if it is the greater (objective) value of the other's life that makes one willing to sacrifice, then each measures the other as greater than himself!

b) Perhaps many people are worth one's life. But does this fit? A fireman would risk his life to save one person as readily as three. Heroism-by-the-numbers isn't heroism.

So we are looking for something larger than any particular human self and larger than even a group of people.

c)Perhaps a principle will do? People might be willing to die for a just wage, fair play, the U.S. Constitution, the Roman Empire, the integrity of Japan, to keep a promise. But each of these (if/as good) is rooted in the good of human persons. Just wages, e.g., are important because actual human beings will draw them and need them and merit them. The value involved in dying for a principle is embedded in the value of persons. So if another human, simply as a human 'object', is not quite enough to die for, then neither are principles rooted in the merely human.

To sum up: It is not fully grounded or relieved of absurdity to be willing to die for i) anything less than a human person ii) one other person considered as a sort of exchange iii) a group of people or iv) something which is part of the good for a group of people.

What's left? Something greater than the human. There might be some intermediate, superhuman reality less than God, but what comes to mind is God*.

Of course, this isn't a proof because we haven't shown that heroism is not absurd. But if it is absurd why do we count these 'absurd ones' as among the highest human beings?

*Not that one dies "for" God in the sense of "boosting" God. But this action calls God to the scene or reveals God in the background with a very dramatic totalness. If so, the analysis holds even for an atheist–his action "speaks louder than thoughts", it eloques (speaks out) a deeper reality.

13. Ground of Science/Truth

A. Science:

For Isaac Newton,[27] God supports the i) existence, ii) method and iii) content of science.

i) God as creator of the world gives it its order and therefore underwrites our study of it. "This most powerful system of the sun, planets, and comets could only proceed from the counsel and dominion of an intelligent and powerful Being." and "The Supreme God is a Being eternal, infinite, absolutely perfect, ..."

ii) The method of the sciences is to 'reason upward' from particular phenomena and experiments to their causes by induction and by further induction and experimentation to more general causes (analysis) and to 'reason downward' from assumed causes to explain phenomena (synthesis). This method cannot be derived from pure logic because the move from particulars to general laws is invalid. You can't get there from here. But it may be justified if there are real causes behind phenomena and if these are ultimately rational and so subject to rational scrutiny. "For it became Him who created them to set them in order. And if he did so it is unphilosophical to seek for any other Origin of the World, or to pretend that it might arise out of Chaos by the mere laws of Nature; ..."

iii) God underwrites space, time etc. Some criticize Newton as making God a "poor tinker" or because a change in theory might drop God. For Newton nature manifests God. He says: "Blind metaphysical necessity, which is certainly the same always and everywhere could produce no variety in things." Finally "And thus much concerning God; to discourse of whom from the appearances of things, does certainly belong to Natural Philosophy."

B. Truth:

There are true propositions such as "The cube, tetrahedron, octahedron, dodecahedron, and icosahedron are the only regular polyhedra." or "All even perfect numbers are of the form $2^{p-1}(2^p-1)$ where p is a prime and $m=2^p-1$, m is a prime". These results are hardly obvious but they can be shown. These don't come to be true, nor are they manufactured by the human mind. Most mathematicians don't feel they are making rules, but discovering things that were "already there"–in other words eternal and necessary truths. If the human mind discovers rather than manufactures truth, it receives it. It feeds on truth. If truth is correlative to mind (truth exists in mind), then there must exist a mind above human mind. Augustine concludes either that this mind is God or if there is something higher yet, then that is God.[28]

Another way to phrase this argument: We have "intuition of truths that are necessary, immutable and absolute." But a floppy contingent being like ourselves can't account for these, for their being necessary, etc. Universal reason won't do–unless it denotes an actual intelligent being. So there must be a necessary and immutable being or mind–God.

[A more complex entry to this argument: The number pi is known to be an "irrational" number–it cannot be written as a fraction, it has an infinite non-repeating decimal expansion. We can ask "Is there a series of a twenty 7's in a row?" somewhere along the series. Some deny that there is an answer to this, apart from the acts that would produce the answer. Others think there must be an answer even if we never find out. Like Columbus coming upon the America that was already there, one finds what is "there" already "in" all-knowing mind.]

14. Meaning

Maurice Blondel[29] opens his book, *Action*, with this: "Yes or no, does human life make sense, and does man have a destiny? I act, but without even knowing what action is, without having wished to live, without knowing exactly either who I am or even if I am." Perhaps a syllogism can be made:

1)Either there is a) ultimate meaning in existence and our lives or b) ultimate absurdity. No middle ground holds.

2)But there are deep meanings in some of the events of life.

3)Since b is false, a is true. (disjunctive syllogism)

The logic is OK here, the premises need defense. Anyone who has experienced a few deep joys will probably accept #2. So the key premise is #1. In the first place, the concept of meaning itself is slippery. Wittgenstein asks "What is the meaning of meaning?".

Leaving this aside, isn't it possible to have some meaning in life even if it ends in emptiness? Islands of light in a sea of darkness?

But can part of a treasure map be helpful if the whole thing communicates nothing or better still if there is no treasure there anyway? Can the bloodshed at Verdun have been worthwhile if World War I was absurd?

I'm told Albert Camus used to spend hours queueing up in front of a movie ticket window. Then just before it was his turn he would walk away. He tests Premise #1 experientially. What is it like waiting in line if you know you aren't going to get a ticket? Camus in the queue is the experimenter. He forces himself to "feel out loud" the absurdity of following through a process with no goal. But if man is a meaning-seeker, in a meaningless world, isn't Camus standing in for all of us?

But if there is ultimate meaning, we can hope that what seems helpless and hurtful will be shown to connect. And for most everyone ultimate meaning is connected to God.

15. Sufficient Reason

For Leibniz a thing must have a sufficient reason for it to exist and for it to be as it is.[30] Everything that comes to be must have an efficient cause to bring it to be and a final cause to give it purpose. Even if the world were eternal, it would require a justification that it does not manifest of itself. A cause must contain enough reality in itself to produce what in fact it does produce (or the principle is violated).

Only God has sufficient reason in Himself. God exists.

[Sufficient Reason goes beyond efficient causality and rational purpose combined. Things have reason not just for their existence, but for their being for the best. If it were better for things to be otherwise, sufficient reason would require that.] So Leibniz claims that God makes the best of all possible worlds. Or rather the best of all com-possible worlds. He admits there are evils and that some things taken in isolation seem far from the best. But taken all together things are for the best. (E.g., we can't have both forced virtue and the good of free will. But compossibly, things are for the best. This is another answer to the problem of evil.)

Some theologians criticize Leibniz as requiring God to create and to create a certain world which makes God a runner-up to Necessity or The Plan. For Leibniz, the point is that God is perfect reason, power and goodness.

16. Ontological Argument

Anselm of Canterbury's argument in the *Proslogion* is called the 'ontological' argument.[31] We cite one version of it: "The fool said in his heart 'There is no God'. But certainly when the same fool hears me say: something-than-which-nothing-greater-can-be-thought (aliquid quo magis nihil cogitari potest) he understands what he hears; and what he understands is in his intellect, even if he does not understand it to be. For it is one thing for a thing to be in the intellect and another thing to understand it to be. When a painter thinks of what he is going to make, he has a thing (the painting) in his intellect. But he does not yet think it exists because he has not yet made it. When he has actually painted it, he has it both in his intellect and he understands that it exists because he has now made it. Even the fool is convinced then that something-than-which-nothing-greater-can-be-thought exists in the intellect since he understands what he hears and what is understood is in the intellect. And certainly that-than-which-a-greater-cannot-be-thought cannot exist in the intellect alone. For if it exists even in the intellect only, it can be thought to exist in reality also, which is greater. Therefore, if that-than-which-nothing-greater-can-be-thought is only in the intellect, this same that-than-which-nothing-greater-can-be-thought is that-than-which-something-greater-can-be-thought. But surely this cannot be. Therefore it is beyond doubt that something-than-which-nothing-greater-can-be-thought exists both in the mind and in reality."

We cast this as follows:
1) The term God is defined as "something than which nothing greater can be thought" or "greatest thinkable"–call it T.
2)To really exist is greater than to exist only in the mind.
3) So if T does not exist, then T' can be thought which has all the properties of T but also exists in reality.

4) Then T'>T.

5) Contradiction, nothing can be thought greater than T.

6) Therefore T or God really exists (not just in thought).

We do allow definitions of things that don't exist. A phoenix is a bird that burns itself up and later arises from its own ashes. In premise #1 he has not yet said God exists. Yet some reject premise #1 saying that we have no such concept or that we have such a concept but it is not God. Kant rejects premise #2, saying existence is not a perfection. Aquinas accepts both #1 and #2 but rejects the argument as an invalid leap from mental or conceptual existence to actual or extramental existence. Descartes, Hegel and others support some kind of ontological argument.

We leave this brain breaker here. If it's wrong, say exactly where. If it's right, try it out on a few friends.

17. Experience/Feeling

> Hagar said, I shall call you EL ROI, for here I
> see the one who sees me.   Gn 13,16

Experience: Everyone counts experience as evidence. A man from Cambodia has never experienced snow. Someone tells him how snow falls, how it feels. This isn't first-hand experience but it does count as evidence that snow exists.

Some times we pick up another's experience most intensely. We are at a party. I hear someone say something insensitive to you. I can tell by your expression that you are very hurt by the remark. If I know you well, I'm awfully sure you're not faking an emotion. Your experience almost becomes my experience as I feel pained for you.

What about someone else's "experience" of God? Mystics claim converse with God, or to have been in His presence or felt showered by God's love. Moses, Rumi, John of the Cross are examples from Jewish, Muslim and Christian religions.[32] This experience is not limited to prophets or religious leaders. Like Bach who felt he was "taking dictation", many 'ordinary' people report "numinous" experience– a contact with God or at least a hyperreal personal something, or an over powering sense that they are doing the right thing or are being called to something.

How to evaluate this kind of experience?

If we know that God doesn't exist then we dismiss it. Some psychology tests ask questions about "seeing visions", "thinking you are in touch with God", etc., and then use "yes" answers for a diagnosis of psychosis.

But for everyone else, why not judge this as we would judge other experience related to us? We look at: i) what is related ii) who is relating it (with what motive, how reliable are they) iii) how they are relating it (are they clear, sincere, on a drug or drunk?).

Obviously the content of such experience is highly charged. It is not quotidian chatter. What if some who speak of experience of God: are of superior intellect; speak with great conviction; keep their "common sense" about other things; are willing to sacrifice; have no "axe to grind"; have actually changed their previous ideas or gone against their earlier desires; "stick to their guns" under pressure or even torture; improve their personality or morality afterwards; etc., etc.?

Any of these adds weight to normal testimony. Several together add great weight.

Feeling: Pascal said the heart has its reasons that reason cannot know. Apart from other approaches there appears to be one based on feeling. For some people it is based on a sense of what has to be, on things that cannot be placed on the table of explanation. Feelings are vague. Mystical experience is much more powerful than a general feeling that there is a "man upstairs". Feelings are not the stuff to build proofs upon–but should they be ignored completely?

18. Anthropological Data/Common Opinion

Anthropology knows no society whose concepts are purely immanent. By purely immanent we mean that they have no notion of any of the following: spirits, souls, demons, objects powered with sacred force, evil forces or places, hexes, afterworlds, underworlds, overworlds, or otherworlds.[33]

Universal opinion is not proof. If everybody denied the circulation of the blood or the existence of germs -so what? Nor does this evidence point directly to God. Some societies seem to have more awe for the awful than a sense of God. The evidence might make a stronger argument for the existence of the chthonic (underworld) than the celestial. But it is heavy evidence that our human condition and cis-worldly (this-worldly) reality are not self-explanatory or self-luminous. If everywhere people are looking elsewhere for explanations, then it looks like the world cannot be explained on its own "plane". Explaining away outside explanations becomes less reasonable.

Possibly the weakest evidence–yet with influence on all of us–is the a) quantity and b) quality of human opinion. a) Most people believe in God. This would be hard to prove as a universal claim, though surveys show it. Let us look at some "hard" cases:

i) India is thought of as a bastion of polytheism, an exception to any general theism. Indeed, India is pullulating with gods. It is hard to find a definitive theology. The Hindu religion has neither historical founder nor definite dogmas. Views range from monism (Sankara); modified monism (Ramanuja); theism (Madhva); devotion to one God (Caitanya, *bhakti*), to many or myriad Gods, to one god while not denying the existence of others (henotheism), or to one god at a time (kathenotheism).

Yet we are told the overwhelming majority of people in India believe God is one and pray to one God through the myriad devotions.

China is thought of as uninterested in God throughout its long history. Yet the ancient sage kings such as the Duke of Chou spoke of a personal God, Shang-Ti (Lord on high) or T'ien (Heaven).[34] Confucius compiled their works in the five books. He claimed to carry forth their teachings in his own work which focused on human social, moral and political relations. Mo Ti taught that the will of God was that we should love all persons. Taoism centers about a transcendent principle Tao (way), sometimes called the "self-so" (tzu-jan).

Some say the Confucian emphasis on harmony goes against God's transcendence and the Tao is simply nothingness or nature. But the Tao as nothing appears to mean no-thing, i.e., not a particular finite entity. In the 16-1700's Matteo Ricci and Emporer K'ang

Hsi claimed that Shang-Ti and Heaven were monotheistic concepts. These things are hard to judge and tell us little about the thoughts or prayers of ordinary people. In any case, these views seem far from atheism.

ii) Some think religion is a matter of the on-going mores or societal pressure or is a prop to the state. Yet in countries where the state or public life is atheistic or anti-theistic many people are theists. But in places with an official religion or theistic public life, there don't appear to be huge pockets of atheists -more Christians in Russia under Lenin or in Mexico under Calles than atheists in Morocco or Ireland or old France.

iii) In fact, religion has proved awfully hard to stamp out. One of the most sophisticated repressions ever was under the Japanese shogun Iesayu Tokugawa. The country was closed and all Christians were forced to convert. Yet 250 years later a pocket of Christians was found in Nagasaki.

b) It is countered that theism is so common only because those with superior intellect are always few. But even if it were true that "most of the godless are intellectuals", it would not follow that "most of the intellectuals are godless". Nor that the most brilliant are. Counting heads is a super-silly way to think (and should raise the supercilia of more than the supercilious) -but if we must: Marx, Freud, Nietzsche, Sartre are well known atheists -add Democritus, Hobbes and Hume. Anaxagoras, Plato, Aristotle, Descartes, Galileo, Kepler, Newton, Locke, Leibniz, Berkeley, Pascal, Planck and Pasteur are theists.

A Coda

An argument subtle, swift and sweeping is made from the distinction between essence and existence. We point out the distinction in three ways:

1"To run" is not the same as "that which runs" so "to be" is not the same as "that which is". "To run" or the "act of running" might also be thought of as that whereby one runs. So "to be" or the "act of existing" (an act not just a fact, nor something stuck on, an accident that 'advenes' to its subject) is also spoken of as that whereby one exists.

"Roger runs" is made up of the subject Roger and the act of running. So a being (ens) is made up of what it is (essence) and the act of existing (esse). The Latin esse, is clumsily, but accurately rendered as "the to be".

2)"Being" or "is" is said in many ways. In "John is the tallest man in the room", the is joins two notions or states a fact, etc. But in "John is", the is has a stronger sense. It points us back to that which underlies all the other actions like running that may be said of John.

[Like much that is primordial, simple or all-embracing, this is easily overlooked. And sentences like "John is" are rare -though grammatical, intelligible and accurate.]

3)We cannot think of an essence without thinking of its intrinsic parts. We cannot think of a triangle without thinking of sides or of an island without thinking of being surrounded by water. But "I can conceive what a man or a phoenix is and still not know whether it has existence" (Aquinas,[36] Being and Essence, ch.4 is the source of the argument). The camelopard was thought not to exist but does (the giraffe); the unicorn met the opposite fate. So existence is not an intrinsic part of essence.

A real being (ens) is composed of what it is (essence) and its "to be" (esse). Is every being so composed?

"Whatever belongs to something is either caused by the principles of its nature, like risibility in man or accrues to it from some extrinsic principle, like light in air, which is caused by the sun." It is impossible that the essence be the cause of the act of existence because then something would produce itself in existence which is absurd. So "every being whose act of existing is other than its essence must have its act of existing from another. And because everything that exists through another is led back to that which exists through itself as to its first cause, there must be one thing which is the cause of existence in all things because it alone is the act-of-being."

By causality we work back to a reality that does not have existence from another -and so is not composed of two principles. In other words, existence is its very essence. Not only must it exist by its very nature, but it is pure existence, unalloyed with any receptive principle. *

The argument may be more abstract than others but it concludes to more -to Subsistent Existence, Reality that stands even if nothing else were.

God is not some empty, formal or general existence, a background or all pervasive quality. Esse commune is the name for the received to-be that beings have. That is not God. God is subsistent existence (esse subsistens). Here it may help to think of Plato's Forms. If e.g., Light Itself existed distinct from all luminous and illuminated objects, it would have all that pertains to light without being scattered, diffused, dispersed, etc. Esse Itself does so exist and has all that pertains to existence -all perfections 'perfectliest' since it has them all as one.

*Is it difficult to think of the to-be in this way? This may help: "I am glad I'm a human, not a pig" or "I wonder what it is like to be a bird" I am not dwelling on a different pig or bird but a different to-be. Again, thinking of being someone else or of being two people at once forces thought back on my to-be, my (received) act of existing.

Footnotes/References

1. Immanuel Kant says speculative natural theology is not possible. See *Critique of Pure Reason* (tr. Norman Kemp Smith, St. Martin's Press, New York 1965). "Thus all attempts to construct a theology through purely speculative reason, by means of transcendental procedure, are without result." p.529.
2. Counters: 1) that God is intensively not extensively infinite 2)evil is a lack and 3)a spatial metaphor does not work -even an infinitely large body need not take up all space, e.g., a body that fills all space except the solar system. This last is of little importance since theists don't think of God as a body.
3. Augustine, *On Free Choice of the Will*, (tr. A.S. Benjamin and L.H. Hackstaff, Bobbs-Merrill, Indianapolis, 1964) p.1 and throughout.
4. J.L. Mackie argues that it is not incoherent to say that God could have created human beings such that they would always freely choose the good. Alvin Plantinga agrees, but claims it is incoherent to say that humans could be caused by God to always freely choose the good. For Mackie the free will defense collapses, for Plantinga

it does not. See J.L. Mackie, *The Miracle of Theism*, (Clarendon Press, Oxford 1982), p.150-176 and Alvin Plantinga, *God, Freedom and Evil* (New York, Harper and Row 1974), pp. 29-55.

The argument has many turns and becomes even more complex as other theological issues are brought in. Theists generally work toward an answer that has some of these elements: a) *culpa* is rooted in man's freedom b) evil is an absence of good not a rival to it (metaphysically, evil is a lack) and c) God draws greater good out of evil. This last might be considered more a hope than a certain claim. Does it have some resonances in our experience, e.g., when deeper friendships and wisdom emerge from our flaws and faults?

5. Others, e.g., Albert Einstein find the mathematical simplicity of nature one of its most compelling features.

6. Lucretius, *De Rerum Natura*, Bk 4, 216-721, 1037-1057.

7. Hobbes, Thomas, *Leviathan*, throughout.

8. Sartre, John Paul, *"Cartesian Freedom" in Literary and Philosophical Essays* (tr. Annette Michelson, Collier, New York 1965) p.189 and Existentialism and Humanism (tr. Philip Mairet, London 1948). See also *Being and Nothingness*.

9. Teresa de (Cepeda y) Ahumada of Avila, *The Life of Teresa of Jesus*, (tr. E. Allison Peers, Image Books, Garden City, NY 1960). I have not found this quote. She and other mystics speak of aridity and a sense of emptiness of God.

10. Freud, Sigmund, *The Future of an Illusion*, (tr. James Strachey, W.W. Norton, New York 1961), p.6. He never tries to disprove God, but simply dismisses the notion. On p.24, he says, "The defense against childish helplessness is what lends its characteristic features to the adult's reaction which he has to acknowledge –a reaction which is precisely the formation of religion."

11. For Sankara see our happiness chapter.

12. Thomas Aquinas, *Summa Theologica*, I, q2, a3. There are many translations. I render these quite literally.

13. Newton, Isaac, *"General Scholium" in the Principia*, (tr. Andrew Motte and Florian Cajori, Univ. of California Press, Berkeley 1973), p.544.

14. Aquinas, ibid. I have rearranged the order of his arguments to put similar arguments together.

15. Frisch, Karl von, *Bees: Their Vision, Chemical Senses,*

and Language (Cornell University Press, Ithaca, NY 1971. A more detailed work is *The Dance Language and Orientation of Bees* (tr. Leigh E. Chadwick, Harvard University Press, Cambridge, MA 1967). To emphasize the complex things going on out in nature I give this quote (selected almost at random from the latter): "Bees do not go flying out at night. But at times there is dancing at night in the hive by "marathon dancers" (*Dauertänzerinnen*), and then one sees that they indicate the direction of the goal to which they flew during the day -as in a dream, one might say- in accordance with the nocturnal azimuth of the sun, concerning which they have no knowledge from experience (pp.351f). They "calculate" the course of the sun's movement, from the west across the north to the east. It has been possible to test other insects and even vertebrates in this regard by observing their nocturnal orientation to an artificial sun. A remarkable finding emerged: some animals act as bees do and let the sun continue its path at night from the west across the north to the east (lizards, fish, some birds, mammals). But others orient as though the sun were to travel in a reversed course from the west across the south to the east. It is thus with Talitrus and Velia, with the beetle Phaleria, and with the wolf spider Arctosa and some birds. We have no explanation for this contrast." p.449. Get it? The bugs do!

16. Thom, René, *Stabilité structurelle et morphogénèse*, InterEditions, Paris, 1977. This is a calculus of discontinuity rather than a study of catastrophes in the normal sense (some radical or rapid change may be for the better). There are seven "elementary catastrophes"–the fold, cusp, swallowtail, butterfly, and the elliptic, hyperbolic, and parabolic umbilics. See also Alexander Woodcock and Monte Davis, *Catastrophe Theory*, Avon, New York, 1980.

17. "Frisch...", is from Richard Wagner's *Tristan und Isolde*, Reclam Stuttgart, 1961, part I lines 6-9. Chuvash is an ethnic group and language in Russia.

18. Darwin, Charles, *Origin of the Species*, New American Library, New York 1958, p.168. See also Francis Hitching, *The Neck of the Giraffe*, Ticknor and Fields, New Haven 1982.

19. Descartes, Rene, *The Philosophical Works of Descartes* (tr. Elizabeth S. Haldane and G.R.T. Ross, Cambridge University Press, London 1973), vol. 1, pp.100-106 and pp.157-171.

20. Al-Farabi [Muhammad Ben Tarkhan Abu Nasr Alfarabi], *The Philosophy of Alfarabi*, Robert Hammond, The Hobson Book Press, New York, 1947, p.21. The quote is given as from The Sources of Questions, p.66.

21. Avicenna [Abu Ali al-Husain ibn Abd Allah also called Ibn Sina], *Avicenna on Theology*, Arthur J. Arberry, Hyperion Press, Westport CN 1979, p.25. The quote is translated from al-Risalat al-Arshiya.

22. Aquinas, *S.T.* I q2a3

23. Adler, Mortimer, *How to Think about God*, Macmillan, New York 1980, pp.131-147.

24. Aquinas, *S.T.* I q2a3.

25. Plato, *Symposium*, 212a, from *The Collected Dialogues of Plato*, ed. Edith Hamilton and Huntington Cairns, Princeton University Press, 1969, p.563.

26. Kant calls the existence of God a 'postulate of pure practical reason'. Duty requires us to promote the summum bonum, but then this must be at least possible, which in turn requires God "it is morally necessary to assume the existence of God." *Critique of Practical Reason*, (tr. Thomas Kingswell Abbott in Kant's Theory of Ethics, London 1889) pp.220-229. See also *Foundations of the Metaphysics of Morals*.

27. Newton, *General Scholium*, pp.543-547 of the *Principia*.

28. Augustine, *On Free Choice of the Will*, pp.35-72. See also Bernardo Bonansea, *God and Atheism*, (CUA Press, Washington, DC, 1979) for a lengthy discussion of this and many other arguments. For the rejection of abstract universal reason as the ground of truth, see Bonansea pp.85-87.

There are questions whose answers are in principle unproduceable. If we have calculated pi to n decimal places, we can ask is there a series of n 7's in a row. Since the first terms are not all 7's, the search must go on. To deny that there is a true answer seems to deny the principle of the Excluded Middle: that a (well delineated) state of affairs either is or is not the case. This is a pillar of logic. See *The Illusion of Technique*, William Barrett, Anchor Doubleday, Garden City 1979, p.104. Would Augustine think this is a strong example of how truth and logic require God?

29. Blondel, Maurice, *L'Action* [1936 version] (Presses Universitaires de France, Paris 1963) p.15. *Action* (1893 version). (tr. Oliva Blanchette, Univ. of Notre Dame Press, Notre Dame, IN 1984 p.3.

30. Leibniz, Gottfried Wilhelm, *Monadology*, #32,38,39. (From G.W. Leibniz, *Discourse on Metaphysics, Correspondence with Arnauld, and Monadology*, tr. George Montgomery, Open Court, LaSalle, IL 1988.

31. Anselm of Canterbury, *Proslogion* II ch.2, tr. M.J. Charlesworth, Univ. of Notre DamePress, Notre Dame, IN, 1979. This is a Latin/English version.

32. Mystical literature is vast. See e.g., *The Classics of Western Spirituality* series, Paulist Press, New York.

33. It is hard to generalize about all cultures -this has been told to me by several anthropologists. For the "actual monotheism" of the people of India I rely on conversations with Hindus and on the testimony of some who have studied or worked there.

34. For Chinese theism see: Legge, James, tr. *The Chinese Classics*, (five vols.) Oxford Univ. Press, New York and London, 1960. Waley, Arthur, tr. *The Analects of Confucius*, Vintage, New York, 1938. Watson, Burton, tr. *Mo Tzu: Basic Writings*, Columbia Univ. Press, New York, 1963. Lao Tzu's Tao Tê Ching is translated by R.B. Blakney as *The Way of Life*, Mentor Books, New York, 1962. For Ricci et al., see The Catholic Encyclopedia articles on *"Chinese Rites Controversy"* and *"Chinese Philosophy"*.

35. Persecutions against and in the name of religion continue. Some even argue against the existence of God on the claim that religion causes evil. They might as well argue for God because of the deeds of some who would extinguish religion.

36. Thomas Aquinas, *De Ente et Essentia*, (On Being and Essence). I have used wordings from translations by: G. Leckie, New York Appleton-Century-Crofts, 1957, R.P. Goodwin, Bobbs-Merrill, Indianapolis, 1965, and Mary T. Clark, *An Aquinas Reader*, Image, Doubleday, Garden City, 1972, p.44, p.111. See also John Wippel's *"Aquinas's Route to the Real Distinction"*, The Thomist, 43, 2, April 1979.

We do not cite further references or raise further questions. The reader or guide is urged to examine carefully these and other arguments.

Quid est ergo tempus? Si nemo ex me quaerat, scio;
si quaerenti explicare velim, nescio.
What is time then? If no one asks me I know;
if I wish to explain it to someone I do not know.
Augustine *Confessions* XI ch 14

TIME

One definition: Time is the measure of change with respect to
before and after. Aristotle (Physics 220a25)
Paradox #1   We use time to measure motion and motion to
measure time.

We presume to know time when we measure speed (30ft/sec)
but we presume we know motion (pendulum, atomic vibrations) to
measure time (make a clock). (1)

Newton: Absolute time is not the same as the measurement of
time. Absolute time "flows equably without relation to anything
external, and by another name is called duration". It is the same
everywhere and is independent of events -like a 'container of
events'.

Einstein: Time and its measurement are the same. Time is
slowed, if processes (and clocks) are slowed. Simultaneity is relative (whether two events happen at the same time depends on where
you are). Twin paradox -space travelling twin ages less. (2)

Another definition: Time is a kind of spanning of soul or mind.
Example -we understand a spoken sentence only when it is finished, over, gone out of existence. Mind stretches to join the present
(moment of understanding) to what has past (the spoken words)
and perhaps this is time. [Augustine] Time seems to pass differently when you are young or old, sad or happy -is this connected to
a mind's span?

                              past   now   future
The line model of time: <————————•————————>

Paradox #2 The past doesn't exist, the future doesn't exist, the present has no duration. Therefore, time, (or duration) doesn't exist. The song was long. The visit was short. Only the past and future can have duration, yet how can you say that what does not exist is long or short.

Another version of this paradox: Each now is gone the moment it is there. As soon as it is, it is not. If a now hung around, if the present instant endured, we would be in eternity, not time. So present time exists only because it keeps falling out of existence. Strange talk.(3)

> Eternity = the standing now (*nunc stans*)
> Time = the now that flows away (*nunc fluens*)

Many theologians think of God as outside of time in eternity. Some truths (e.g., the Pythagorean Theorem) seem more outside time than in it. We speak in the timeless present when we say '2 and 2 is 4' but not when we say 'France is larger than Germany'.(4)

Heidegger rejects the line model of time and claims that measured or 'physics' time is a derived and inferior sense of time (inauthentic temporality). Authentic temporality joins the three parts. When we decide (presentish), we shape what can be, what is open to us (futurish), out of what we are, what has been, what options there are (pastish). (5)

We find time fascinating, but so obscure that we have pulled the rest of even this tiny discussion out to the end as a kind of "extra for experts".

---

(1) Solution?: We use motion to measure time to measure another motion. So really we use motion to measure motion. That is we use regular motion (pendulum, atomic vibrations) to measure irregular motion (how long it takes to get home). But how do we tell that the regular motion is regular? Suppose the earth's rotation is being slowed. Then the length of a day is increasing. But how would we know?

Newton might say that we correct measurements of time by setting them against a more accurate measurement. But doesn't this process of getting more accurate point to something like an 'independent duration' which serves as a background against which change can be contrasted?

(2) The night of their high school graduation (time A), one twin (Rebecca) goes on a high speed space trip. She rejoins her twin (Roberta) on earth at their fiftieth reunion (time B). The earth bound twin is gray and stoop-shouldered. Her grandchildren are serving the drinks. The space voyager twin says it's been a great year. Her watch shows it, her looks show it, and she is looking forward to college. This is the twin paradox -a consequence of the special theory of relativity. If this is true, there can be less duration between the same two times.

∧∧∧∧∧∧∧∧∧∧∧∧

A_____B

So the 'paths' between the A and B are different. Einstein would rejoin simply that each person has his own time (which he has in common with others as long as they are not moving too fast and not too far away). Time, simultaneity and space are different for each one.

Of course, there are times that seem to fly and times that seem to drag -but we accept that we were wrong when told what time it is. Here no such correction is possible.

In any event, doesn't this make nonsense out of treating time as a graphable, physical-mathematical quantity or as a dimension [which seems to underlie the physics of both Einstein and Newton]?

(3) Heraclitus says '*panta rhei* ', everything flows. You cannot step into the same river twice. Such is existence; such is life. But is he speaking of the change in us and in things more than about an abstraction called time? Can difficulties in speaking about time be relieved if we move the discussion to the changing things? The now slips away, runs off, because things keep changing. Is the radical evanescence of us, and all about us, the root mystery? But what if things stayed the same for a while -would it make sense to ask if it was for a long or a short time? [4] Some distinguish between ever-lastingness or infinite time or endless duration or '*aeviternity*' and eternity. Boethius says, "Eternity is the whole, simultaneous and perfect possession of boundless life." For Aquinas the eternal is being-all-at-once (tota simul existens). Parmenides speaks of the

One or Being as "all at once a single whole".

There is no succession in eternity. The standing now is outside time, outside infinite duration. Aristotle's world is everlasting rather than eternal. It is forever changing.

What about yet two other cases? Can you conceive of something that begins to be but never ends? Some of us would volunteer to be just such an example. If we began to be and if there is personal immortality, then we fit the case.

We illustrate it: •——————————>

Some find this unthinkable and say either that soul(s) always are (transmigration, reincarnation) or that what began must end, so there is no aevum (the word sometimes used for this type of reality).

Can you think the flip side of this?: A being that has already existed for an infinite duration but that will cease to exist on December 31, 1999 or somesuch?!

I find I cannot conceive of such, yet I can easily draw a symbol for it:

<——————————•

This too is strange. [If you can conceive the former but not the latter, does this weaken the claim that what begins must end since the cases are not symmetrical?]

(5) Heidegger faces down the problem of speaking a new theory about time without using the old time words, but the price is high - the difficult time people have reading *Being and Time*. 'Past' is replaced by 'having been', 'thrown'. Our existence is always already there. Life and its conditions are things thrown at you. Red hair. Brown eyes. Born in the twentieth century. The future is the 'to come'.

The present is the moment. The German word for moment is Augenblick -a blink of the eye. [Heidegger loves to draw on etymologies.] One more special usage: Ecstasy literally means 'standing out of'. Time is the horizon of our being. Authentic man draws time into himself. So he has time for things. Plenty of time. Inauthentic man doesn't have time for things, can't make time. In this mode, time is always running down, running out.

As we said earlier, the three aspects of time are drawn together especially in the moment of decision. In a triumphal shout near the end of the book, Heidegger says that only a being that is futural and finite can take over its own 'thrownness', hand down to itself its own past and, in the moment of vision (blink-of-the-eyeingly!), be for its own time. He calls this 'joining' the triple ecstasy. Is there a one of which these three are parts, or from which past, present and future stand out? His thought may be like the Christian doctrine of the Trinity -in which there are three persons but no fourth which is their sum or whole.

There is sprung energy and deep resonance in Heidegger's call to be real, to stand up, to surpass our very boundedness or fate in the act of accepting and deciding.

But what does it all come to? Is it happy?

If we draw the future in each case out of the treasure trove of the given (the past), where is anything truly new? Where's hope? [Heidegger appears to relate hope to the expectation of getting some already-known (pastish) goody for oneself.]

No matter how superreal a big deciding may make us feel or be, is it enough? Is the point of deciding simply to decide? Is decision hyperreal because it is for the sake of decision itself? Or is decision/choice aimed at something, at 'objects', at things and persons loved? Could there be reality that truly is 'ecstatic' and new for us? Do these comments touch his idea of time or other ideas?

Before deciding that time is a hopeless case, let us glance toward Edmund Husserl. If I understand correctly, he distinguishes three levels: i) external physical objects that take time, like a game or a song; ii) inner objects such as sensations, intentional acts etc.; iii) inner time consciousness.

The now of perception (level ii) is not an atomic now–it is attended by retentions and protensions. The binding together of these is a slice of the flow of consciousness. This deepest level is what makes remembering possible.

In remembering, we don't bring up a little picture, which, though itself a present reality, is somehow inscribed with a past date. We have the thing or event itself, together with the experience of remembering it. We do not represent, we re-present.

This parallels the way we perceive. We perceive the physical object itself (not a tiny mental xerox of it) and experience that we are perceiving it. Inner time consciousness is the ground that makes this kind of thing possible. It has more than one track. I am listening to my child and myself a child hearing my father. You are doing the dishes and walking through the cherry blossoms in Washington, D.C. We can be awarefully and competently attending to both.

We might ask whether inner time consciousness is most fundamental? If consciousness is always consciousness of something, does this dance us back to things -where the notions of time got so mysterious in the first place?

Exactly what inner time consciousness is and how it is related to self, other selves, the philosophical viewpoint, etc., we must leave for further study.

Some key references are:

Aquinas, *Summa Theologica*, I, q10
Aristotle, *Physics, De Memoria et Reminiscentia*
Augustine, *Confessions,* Book X and XI
Boethius, *The Consolation of Philosophy,* Cons. V, Part VI
Einstein, *Relativity: The Special and the General Theory.*
Hegel, *Phenomenology of Spirit*
Heidegger, *Being and Time,* see esp. p.437 (Macquarrie tr.)
Heraclitus, *Fragment 49a*
Husserl, *The Phenomenology of Internal Time Consciousness*
Newton, *Principia,* pp.6-12 [Scholium]
Parmenides, *Fragment 8*
Michael Chester gives an analysis of the twin paradox in *Relativity*, W.W.Horton, New York, 1967. We do not assume that either theory of relativity is true.

Kathleen Freeman has translated Diels, *Fragmente der Vorsokratiker* in *Ancilla to the Pre-Socratic Philosophers*, Harvard Univ. Press, 1966

Robert Sokolowski's *Husserlian Meditations* (Northwestern University Press, Evanston, 1974) is very clearly written and has excellent examples. I recommend it to those who wish to get a "purchase" on Husserl. See p. 138-168 especially.

Many questions are in the text -a few others here.

1) Time takes us to memory. Study one of the theories of memory. What is remembering? Why do we forget or misremember? In what sense do/don't we control what we remember?

2) Why is time primarily viewed as negative. In "Fern Hill", Dylan Thomas says it held him "green and dying" and calls it "chains". Is it because of aging and death? Or is something else involved?

3) Is it conceivable that there be a human keeping-in-existence which is not duration as we now know it? Put another way -if there is everlasting life for us, will we always be looking forward to the next thing, to something happening? [What would the opposite be?]

4) Try to think of time for "lower beings", rocks or living things with little or no memory.

5) Try to think of time for "higher beings"–beings of much deeper, more intense and rapid intellection and choice, perhaps. Could they be above our kind of time? Have some aspects of it in common with us? Etc.

6) In what sense does love affect time? Does it gather up its parts intensely? Does it make duration itself a positive thing? Why should it have any affect at all?

7) Think on what existence outside time could be like. Try to describe it in some way. Is there anything in our experience that could help here?

Roseau pensant.
A thinking reed.
Le silence éternel de ces espaces infinis m'effraie.
The eternal silence of the endless spaces frightens me.
[Pascal, *Pensées*, 113,201]

IMMORTALITY

I. Introduction

Is the soul immortal? Will we rise again? What is out there for us in the after-death? Will I see my folks, my friends? Or is it as Ernest Dowson fears:

"They are not long the weeping and the laughter,
Love and desire and hate:
I think they have no portion in us after
We pass the gate."

Vitae summa brevis spem nos vetat incohare longam, lines 1-4

These questions aren't all the same. The resurrection of the body isn't just some general consciousness surviving. Our main interest is personal immortality–do I survive death?

Those who believe there is no life or personal awareness beyond the grave usually leave the burden of proof to the other side. For them, death seems so overpoweringly final that a theoretical defense of mortality is not called for.

Most people know Christianity and Islam promise life after death, but they may not realize that arguments have been put forth apart from faith. Nor do the faithful agree–Avicenna and Aquinas hold that personal immortality is demonstrable; Scotus believes in it, but does not think it can be proven.

Some view anyone who takes an afterlife seriously as emotionally immature or perhaps even neurotic. Yet others base their reasonings for immortality on psychology itself (in the sense of the science of the psyche or soul) or on the structure of the human.

Modus quo corporibus adhaerent spiritus comprehendi ab hominibus non potest, et hoc tamen homo est.
[How the spirit is united to the body cannot be understood by man–and yet it is man.] Augustine, *City of God* xxi 10

Among philosophers who 'favor' immortality, many think proving it a hard problem since it involves descriptions of human structure -how we know or think, how mind or soul are with body, what we are. And this, for some mysterious reason, is mysterious. Others derive immortality from morality.

Doctrines of the after life that come from faith or private experience lie outside philosophy's scope -but we can look at what leads up to them and what follows from them.

II. Survey of Arguments

We outline seven 'tents' or families of views. On the surface, at least, within each tent there is much in common. But first we introduce four terms that are critical to the logic of soul-talk. A *substance* is something that exists in itself, like a horse. An *accident* is something that inheres in another like whiteness in a horse. A leg or an ear is *part* of a horse. The *form* is the essence or the 'what' of a thing or what makes it to be that kind of thing. A form is not a part. Form characterizes or permeates the whole.

A. Plato/Descartes

A) Plato and Descartes have very different philosophies but they both have a wide divide between body and soul. [Plato wears many masks and talks on many levels–we look at his arguments here on a fairly literal level.] If, as Plato says, the soul is in the body like a pilot in a ship or a man in prison, or if the body is like a coat wrapped around the soul, then it is not surprising that the soul survives death. He argues:

1. Among movers, those that move themselves and others are prior to those that merely are moved by others. Soul is the former.

2. Soul or mind uses the body. Senses are instruments. We see through the eyes more than with them. At best, the eyes might be credited with seeing two like things but not that they are alike.

Likeness, truth, justice are perceived in/by soul alone.
3. Scientific explanations don't get to the root of things. If we ask why Socrates is here, science only explains the physiology of his motion, not the reason why he stays rather than chooses exile. Natural science stays on the level of physical causation -how, not why. Only mind has purpose. Soul is prior to, superior to and sovereign over body.
4. In many places Plato speaks of the struggle mind has controlling the body. This points to two principles in us. Suppose someone is having a hard time quitting smoking. He experiences a division of sorts. He might say "I want to quit, but the urge (my body) gets in the way. He doesn't say "I don't want to quit but my mind gets in the way." He doesn't root for the triumph of body over mind, but lines the "I" up with mind/soul/judgment.

Descartes sets out to build a secure foundation for science as technology. To clear the ground and make his principles certain, he tries to doubt all he can. He can think himself bodiless and feign the world annihilated. But in doing all this he comes up against his own thinking. *Cogito ergo sum.* I think therefore I am. The vividness of consciousness and self-consciousness overcome doubt and drive him to affirm mind/soul as an unextended thinking substance, the polar opposite of body which is extended and unthinking. Bodies are automata–indeed he claims that is what animals are. But he cannot extend this to man.

For Descartes, one problem is the unity of man. How do body and soul add up to one person, how do they interact -it seems certain they do interact: colors affect moods; moods affect health; brain has a lot to do with thinking; etc! For Plato, we can ask about the individual soul–is what survives me?

B. Aristotle

For Aristotle, soul is the first principle of a living thing. A living thing is quite different from the 'same' thing not living. It is a one and not merely a congery of neighboring parts, a heap. What makes an orange or an okapi be and act as a one is its overall organizing principle or form. Without form the *"Pieta"* is merely a condominium of calcium carbonate crystals and we are a series of cells.

Nutrition, locomotion, sight are principles of living things, but the eye of a dead man doesn't see, so soul is the first principle of a living thing.

If we use the word soul for the form of a living thing, then there must be souls. Animals and plants have soul but of a different order than ours. Aristotle would never agree that animals are automata (neither would any pet or vet), which seems to follow if you deny them soul.

If the human person is a one, and if we think, imagine, remember, will–then the unifying principle of man must include these. Man has thinking soul. The more high-powered the living thing, the more high-powered its soul.

But if the soul is the form of the body, then it is tied intimately to this particular body. The disintegration of the body carries the soul along with it, just as the melting of a wax figure carries off its funny face.

This does appear to be Aristotle's view and it does follow cleanly on the notion of the soul as simply the form of the body. Further, for Aristotle, it is an axiom that what begins to be must cease to be. Yet that is not his very last word. He left us this cryptic paragraph:

"Mind in the passive sense becomes all things, but mind has another aspect in that it makes all things; this is a kind of positive state like light; for in a sense light makes potential colors into actual colors. Mind in this sense is separable, impassive and unmixed, since it is in essence an activity; for the agent is always superior to the patient, and the originating cause to the matter. Actual knowledge is identical with its object. Potential is prior in time to actual knowledge in the individual, but on the whole it is not prior in time. Mind does not think at one time and at another not. When isolated, it is its true self and nothing more, and this alone is immortal and everlasting (we do not remember because, while mind in this sense cannot be acted upon, mind in the passive sense is perishable), and without this nothing thinks." (430a14-25).

What is he talking about? There is an extended analogy between thinking and seeing. I walk into a dark room that has a painting on the wall. My sense of sight is potential sighting and the painting is potential colors, but there is no (actual) sighting. I flip on the light and both sighting and colors are actual. But how does this explain what he calls *nous poetikos*–making or active mind. Light doesn't make the picture! How is light separable? How do we flip it on? Do we each have our own making-mind? How does this relate to paying attention and to thinking continuously?

Before going on, we have a dilemma: 1) If soul is 'far apart' from body, it is easy to show it is deathless but hard to show it is the same person <immortality without identity>. 2) If soul is intimately joined to body, there is no problem of personal unity but it is hard to show it survives death <identity without immortality>. Neither gives what we want.

Are there arguments that do? We give Avicenna's short and Aquinas's long argument that individual soul is immortal.

C. Avicenna/Aquinas

The Persian/Arabic metaphysician and physician Ibn Sina is known to the West through his Latin name, Avicenna. He claims that when I say "I perceived and became angry" it is the same who perceives and gets angry. This centralizing principle cannot be the body as a whole (hands and feet are obviously not meant) nor even any special part (in which case only that part of us perceived and became angry). The faculty which combines both is soul -immaterial and individual.

Michael Marmura (in The Encyclopedia of Philosophy article on him) says, "If a man were to come into being fully mature and rational but suspended in space so that he was totally unaware of his physical circumstances, he would still be certain of one thing - his own existence as an individual self." Do modern sensory deprivation experiments have anything to say about Avicenna's thought experiment?

In arguing against transmigration, Avicenna says that each of us "is conscious that he has a unique soul that governs and controls him." The body is the soul's instrument which the soul uses to perfect itself by getting speculative knowledge. [The soul can also be perfected if one lives a pure life.]

Thus the soul is immaterial and individual. As such it does not perish by falling into parts (since it is immaterial) nor (as a form does) when something else is destroyed (since it is more like an individual substance). This guarantees for Avicenna, not the resurrection of the body, but life everlasting–personal immortality.

For Aquinas, intellectual soul is the form of the body. Soul itself is not another bodily part. If it were it could not be what makes a body act as one thing. Soul is not a little motor, but is present in every part of the body as a form is. Despite divisions and separations, man appears to be one being. It is the same I who think, am glad, sad, tired, shy, amused, who walk, eat, run, reflect. The thinking power seems to be one with the human soul. We have an intellectual soul.

It is intellectual soul that most truly is man and that makes him to be one and himself. For if two men were joined so that they had but one eye, there would be two seers but only one sight. But if one man touches two different things there is one toucher and two touchings. So the one who acts (agent) is most identified with intellectual soul or mind.

[We don't say that a man is soul, rather he is the composite. Exactly how intellectual soul is united to the body is a deep and unfinished subject. Many deny soul or use it to mean other things. But it is hard to deny mind, because we need it to deny it. Pondering hovers over the relation between mind and soul and between soul and body.]

We can reflect on our own experience of ourselves. It is the same self in each case–or else how could I hope for something tomorrow if the person to whom it comes won't be me? Although language is public and is intimately related to thought, each man does have his own intellect.

Thoughts are not material things. Thoughts do not take up space or have weight in an ordinary sense. The thought of a heavier stone is not a heavier thought. The thought of Andorra does not have to be wedged between the thought of Spain and the thought of France.

We know some timeless truths. We come to know them in time, but when we understand we realize they are timelessly true. For example: A perfect number is the sum of all its factors including 1 but not the number itself. So $6 = 1+2+3$ is perfect. $28 = 1+2+4+7+14$ is the next perfect number. It may take a while to find that 496 is the next perfect number. Your discovery happens in time, but you simultaneously realize that back in the Paleozoic days 496 was the third perfect number. Is there an odd perfect number? If this comes to be known, it won't come to be true. Rather we are in a realm of the timelessly and universally true.

All material things are individual or particular.

If mind were a material thing it should understand only individual things. The eye sees only individual triangles but the mind knows triangles in general. The geometer depends on diagrams to reach and teach his theorems. But the theorems are not precisely about the near-triangles or near-circles he may draw. They are true only of the perfect and general circles he can never draw. These are grasped by the mind.

The thinking power works through the body but goes beyond it in its grasp of general truths and in reflection.

We have two categories:

material	in space	thoughts	not spatial
physical	in time	and	not time-bound
things	individual	intellect	general

I know a theorem and know that I know it. Reflection involves a kind of doubling back or double. Each material thing is in a single space and time. So reflection goes beyond any merely material entity.

He gives another example: After seeing a bright light or hearing a loud noise we are less able to sense what is dimmer or quieter. The intense input temporarily uses up the corporeal organ. But when we study or think intensely on some topic, immediately afterward less abstruse concepts seem transparent, super easy. So thinking is not related to brain as seeing is to eye. Intellect is not a corporeal organ.

As a thing acts or operates so it is. If intellectual soul acts beyond the capacities of the merely physical, of the body to which it is united here and now -then it may exist beyond it. Since what-it-is-to-be-me is mostly intellectual soul, then what is me-most may exist beyond bodily death.

Consider how something may cease to be. Only three ways seem possible: 1) it may break into parts, 2) it may perish as a whole indirectly, 3) it may perish as a whole directly.

1) Breaking up of parts. A building is taken apart. The house no longer exists. But if intellect or soul is a form, not a material thing, it doesn't have such parts.

2) Perish indirectly: The form of a thing goes out of existence when the thing itself dies or is destroyed. The snowman dies when the snow melts, the shape and smile of the wax figure when the wax is heated. This is how forms die. The smile is in the shape and the shape in the solid wax. The shape must be the shape of something.

Many people fear their death will be as the snowman's. They may grant that there is soul or something like it. They certainly grant consciousness or mind. But they feel that all this will be as the silly face of a summer snowman.

These forms have no independent operation. But if human soul already has acts beyond the limits of mere body even when joined to body, it is not so dependent, so embedded.

3) Perish directly: This is annihilation, going straight into nothingness. The laws of science preclude this for normal change. It would seem that only what can bring something into being from nothing (no previous being) can send a thing into nothing (a residue of zero). If so, then only God the creator could annihilate. But God seems least likely to do so.

So if each soul is a form that can also stand on its own and God does not annihilate it, it is immortal.

A form that has activities of its own is unlike anything else in either physical nature or the spirit world. We are unique. If so, could that be why it is so difficult to think about our own reality - we are different in kind from the world around us, the world from which we draw the analogies and metaphors that shape our understanding and speech.

A problem for Aquinas is this: how is the intellectual principle the same as the form of the body. The thing that is subsistent (can stand on its own) must be the same as the thing that is the form for the argument to hold. If they are two, then the argument is a hybrid and tends to unravel.

To sum up his long argument: Man is a unified being. Each has his own intellectual soul. Even in this life intellect has some operations that go beyond the scope of brain/body e.g., reflection. As a thing operates so it is. Thus, intellectual soul can exist beyond death, because it can operate beyond body. Aquinas adds that it is incomplete without body. His hope for completeness is in the resurrection of the body.

D. Materialism

Materialism takes many forms. It seems to us a very modern view -who in a biology class talks about soul?- but it is ancient too. Let us look at what might be two extremes: One views man as a robot, the other a most advanced animal.

Think of a simple type of structure, a tinkertoy. It is a structure, it has characteristics that the individual parts don't. But it lacks any controlling nucleus, any true center, organizing principle, inner hierarchy. I know of no one who thinks of man in exactly these terms. But there are conceptions of the human that are close to extensions of this model. Some think science will draw us closer to such self-understanding.

A computer has a hierarchy of sorts but no inner world, no immanence. What it does is a complicated, but exact reflection of what is done to it. It can be slow but it cannot be shy. Compare a computer to a cow. Computers act smart but are dumb. They can be damaged but they can't be hurt. Some people consider the human brain as the main thing about us and they think of the brain as a megacomputer. If their ideas are combined and if their notions of what is possible to technology come to fruition -it is hard to see where they would put an essential difference between man and computer. B.F. Skinner's psychology comes close to this.

Other views pull back from such mechanical description. They see the individual human organism as what we mean by a person. And they see persons as very special. But they do not feel there is anything spiritually unique to man. And they view mind, consciousness, etc. as epiphenomena, as riders on the high biological structures we happen to have.

At an extreme they may even grant a kind of soul in the sense of a seat of feeling, personality, or perhaps as a harmony of parts. But they would never consider intellect as a trans-physical something. Often they view thoughts as generalized responses from individual cases and tend to undermine absolute and eternal truths or limit them to mathematics or deny universals and a faculty capable of conceiving them. The opposite idea is considered as metaphysical voodoo that holds to some sort of inner man behind the man I am shaking hands with.

We are lumping ideas and not giving names. But these ideas come in many flavors and are in no short supply. Epicurus says that we are by the coming together of atoms and we cease at their dissolution. Hobbes speaks of desire, etc. in terms of little mechanical pings and pangs. Hume works to undo the universality of mathematics and denies the self.

All these deny any part, form or substance that survives death. Each theory would have to be examined separately. They may account well for the psycho-physical unity of man. If mind and body are not different in kind, it is easier to explain their interaction. A problem here is to account for the "I", for the kind of inner appearings emphasized by Avicenna, Aquinas, or Descartes. Some say that inner experience is merely private and not material for public proof. Another problem is the adequacy of any account of man that does not include an account of his own accounting.

E. Kant

A good person seeks to do what is right because it is right. Duty commands us to act in such a way that our action can be made a universal maxim. I cannot have one set of rules for myself and another for everyone else. One who acts out of duty may not be happy, but he deserves to be happy.

[So there ought to be a God to give this happiness.] But knowing happiness will soon run out, infects it with sadness. No joy is full if we know it will end even in the distant future. [In the Critique of Practical Reason (pt 1, book 2, ch 2, pt iv), Kant argues for immortality because we need an endless progress from lower to higher forms of moral perfection. Here the argument is linked to the attainment of the happiness the good agent deserves.]

So personal immortality is required if morality is to make sense. That is, there ought to be God and there ought to be immortality. But what is the status of these oughts?

Kant's morality is meant to be a purely rational one - free of custom, exception, revelation, etc. and the same for all rational agents. God and immortality are needed -or else rational morality is irrational. [See also this argument for the existence of God.]

F. Resurrection of the Body

We get back the same transformed body (some of us hope it will be greatly transformed!) or, at least, a body especially related to the same 'me'. What happens between death and bodily resurrection? Various answers are given (immortality of the soul being one). There must be some connection between the "I" who live on earth and the "I" who is resurrected or the idea is more of a re-creation than a resurrection.

Some people find this notion unimaginable. Its adherents do not claim to give a philosophical proof, though they might argue that it fits well with human aspirations, with the moral sense, or that it is a widely held notion (ancient Egypt), etc. But a lack of proof is not an absurdity. The philosophical underpinning would be that what God has made, God can restore. That He actually restore or renew or reward is to be taken on faith, but not against reason.

G. Reincarnation

If the soul upon death becomes the soul of another being, it must be the kind of thing that can do so. What kind of thing is that? Many descriptions have been given. Soul is usually viewed as substance-like.

Some people claim to remember past lives or to speak ancient languages they never learned in this life. This is not the place to weigh those claims but we do note that they are given as empirical evidence. [After death experiences are given as evidence also. Rather than dismiss any evidence, we urge that it be examined carefully as to what happened and what exactly it is evidence for.]

Another appeal of this view is that a given lifetime often seems too short to express the person -would he have been kind, brave? Given his talents what would he have done?

Theories vary on whether reincarnation will go on forever and how the soul has existed previously.

One idea that is incompatible with reincarnation is that the soul is the form of the body or elsewise uniquely tied to this body. Apart from bodily connection, reincarnation goes against personal individual identity, if it claims that what we take to be two different people (e.g., Tutankhamen and Elvis Presley) have the same soul. This may be another contrast: Karma is the moral credit or debit acquired in this life. Most reincarnation theories hold that this is carried over to the next incarnation and indeed is one of the reasons for needing many lives. In Christianity divine forgiveness breaks karma. One Incarnation suffices to give it and one incarnation to receive it.

Some key references are:
   Aquinas, *Summa Theologica,* I, q75-79
   Aristotle, *De Anima*
   Avicenna, *Avicenna's Psychology* (tr. F. Rahman, Hyperion
      Press, Westport, CN, 1981). See also the article on him in
      the Encyclopedia of Philosophy by Michael Marmura.
   Descartes, *Discourse on Method*
   Kant, *Critique of Practical Reason* and *The Foundations of
      the Metaphysics of Morals*
   Plato, *Phaedo, Meno, Theaetatus, Phaedrus, Republic*

For reincarnation, see Hindu or Buddhist scriptures. For the Christian and Muslim notions of the resurrection see the New Testament and the Koran. For an investigation of some of its aspects, see Aquinas, *ST I*, q89 and *III* (supplement).

If the burden is on the affirmative, we can leave the negative side alone.

Questions: Think deeply on what we are and what it means.

Free–from Gothic *frijon*, to love. *Servants or slaves were bound; members of the family were loved and so, free.*

FREEDOM

I. Introduction

II. External Freedom

III. Internal Freedom
  1. Kinds
  2. Arguments for
     A. Experience
     B. Duns Scotus
     C. Modus Tollens
  3. Arguments against
     A. Physical Determinism
        a. Calculability
        b. Force/Energy
     B. Psychological Determinism
        a. Non-conscious
        b. Conscious
     C. Theological Determinism
        a. Causality
        b. Knowledge

IV. Footnotes and References

V. Questions

I. Introduction

There are two kinds of freedom: freedom to carry out, get, or do what you want and freedom to want in the first place. The former we call external freedom, the latter internal freedom.

II. External Freedom

Freedom to walk out the door, say what you please, dress as you wish or travel where you want -these are all external freedoms. In each case, the wanting is assumed and consideration turns to being able to do the thing. Many things may limit external freedom -lack of money, physical limits, the coercive power of the state, the gossip of neighbors, the opposing desires of other people, limited choices or knowledge of choices, infirmities of the body, the realities of nature and constraints of existence itself.

I want to leave but I am chained to the wall.

You want an expensive dress but can't pay for it.

He can't order because he doesn't know the language.

I want to fly, be invisible, have existed forever.

The oceans of discussion about freedom are usually about external freedom. Much of politics and economics is about fitting freedom in with other goods -safety, health, peace, equality, fraternity, someone else's freedom. Practically every new law restricts some freedom in the name of a common good or individual right, although some laws or rulings do the opposite -extend a freedom against the constraints of custom, other laws, rights, freedoms or even other lives. There are many quarrels about freedoms. Should a person be free to express hatred for his country or another race, to teach falsehoods, to constrain others from doing evil, to enter and leave any country he wishes?

How shall we even speak of freedom? Is public school free because children don't have to pay for it, or are the children unfree because they have to go and have to submit to state-mandated curricula? Is television free because we don't have to put coins in it, or is it unfree because only a narrow band of opinions are ever expressed? Perhaps some freedoms we think we have are manipulated illusions. And the converse?-could we think we are constrained when in fact we are free as can be?

No matter how we resolve such, they do not reach to what freedom is or whether it is. We turn to this -a relatively complex discussion -but one necessary if we are even to begin to take hold of central issues.

III. Internal Freedom

1. Kinds

Three senses of internal freedom are distinguished:

a) Sovereignty or mastery: I freely wish X in the sense that this willing is from me, it flows from what/who I am. This highlights a lack of external coercion. A tree growing in an open field grows more freely than one confined against a wall. A brick in free fall is not constrained. So how the tree grows or how the brick falls comes partly from its own nature or what it is. Human behavior that springs from human nature is free in this way. I freely wish to live and freely want to be happy. This is the weakest of the three senses since we can speak of natural things as free in this way.

b) Otherwiseness or free choice: I freely wish to go to city X but could have chosen to go to city Y. I choose apples but could have chosen pineapples. This includes sovereignty but goes beyond it -it must be possible to wish or choose otherwise.[Some thinkers say wanting to be happy is free, in sense a, but not in sense b. They distinguish the voluntary from free-choice.[1] If there is a good that completely fills up or exhausts the desiring capacity, then the desire for that is voluntary but not a free choice. Free choice occurs only between finite goods on the way to happiness. Example: I cannot want otherwise than not to be hungry but I can freely choose a ham or beef sandwich to overcome that hunger.]

c)Spontaneity: Not only does the wanting come from me, not only could I have wished something else instead, but this wish issues purely or almost purely out of me (almost as an uncaused whim). This kind of freedom involves a minimum of being acted upon. Here you don't love a thing because something astonishing or lovely about it tugs on you. Rather the love or wanting confers excellence or value–you dub the thing good! Human choice for Jean Paul Sartre[2] and God's choice to create for Aquinas are examples given for this.

Spontaneity freedom includes mastery and free choice. Is it too extreme? Is it possible for humans who have bodies of a definite composition? Can I make myself hate strawberries or love brussels sprouts by a mere act of the will?

The three kinds arranged in order of intensity are:

spontaneity > otherwiseness > mastery

Most people mean free choice when they talk of free will. However arguments about freedom can be subtle and do not affect all kinds equally, so we distinguish carefully.

2. Arguments for

A. Experience

We experience freedom. We feel we could have done otherwise. We did it because we wanted to. You stopped to give me a ride because you are kind. I did it for the hell of it. It is up to me. I know it was my fault.

We also experience a difference between the automatic behavior of things or the very predictable behavior of plants and animals and the help and hurt that comes from people, from therefore, human internal freedom.

B. Duns Scotus

John Duns, better known as Duns Scotus, claims that we are directly aware of freedom.[3] There is contingency in the world. If someone denies this, Scotus facetiously suggests he be exposed to torments until he concedes that it is possible for him not to be tormented. Not everything exists by necessity. As we are aware of contingency in things, so we are aware of our own freedom.

Freedom of the will is unique. [For Scotus, contingency in the world also points out God's free will in making a world.] Other potentialities are determined both as to whether and how they act - e.g. whether the volcano will explode and how much lava will emerge. We, however, choose one or another possibility or refrain from willing at all.

Scotus elaborates another distinction: The will has two affections or inclinations. The *affectio commodi* is the inclination to what is to our own completion and perfection; the *affectio justitiae* is an inclination to justice or a love of something 'for its own sake', according 'to its intrinsic worth', for 'what it is in itself'

This latter aspect of volition insures its sovereignity over natural controls: physical coercion, psychological compulsion or even the tendency to seek one's own perfection.

We notice the affectio justitiae in the 'tendency to make others admire the beautiful, or the sorrow felt when perfectly lovely things are unloved or desecrated'. It allows a love above jealousy and takes us into the spiritual stratosphere where we can love the most sublime reality regardless of any payoff in it for ourselves. Thus, Scotus offers a different solution to the "problem of selfishness" (See the chapter on love.).

C. Modus Tollens

This is the name given to the logical structure:

A implies B, not B, therefore not A

That is, we look at a position (A) not by analyzing it directly, but by looking at its consequences (B). If the consequences have to be rejected, then so does the original position. What follows if we deny human internal freedom?

The ordinary exchanges of human life and love are founded on internal freedom. Certainly the talk about them is. From the simplest thanks to the most vicious gossip, the praise and blame we get and hand out express the idea that wishes and acts flow freely from us. No one forces us to be kind or snobby.

If there be no freedom, guilt and shame are bleached out. But so are patience and humor, tenderness and bravery. The peaks and valleys of us are bulldozed flat.

My car conks out due to an electrical problem. I pull to the side of the highway. Many drivers go right by, ignoring my pleas for assistance. Finally one fellow stops and gives me a lift. I feel very thankful and tell him so. But what if I think the man really had no freedom–his stopping was just like my car's stopping, only harder to analyze!

A fuse blows and saves the wiring from setting a house on fire. A man puts out an incipient fire at great risk to himself. The two results are similar but the realities are spoken of very differently, because they are so different. No one sends a thank-you note to a fuse!

This is the modus tollens argument. Rejecting the consequences of determinism we restore internal freedom. Deeply rooted as our tie to internal freedom is in ordinary and practical life, its theoretical defense is a much more difficult matter. There are many powerful arguments whose consequences are that the fireman is no freer than the fuse. If we reject this consequence -in our actions and speech and then in our reflections on such -then we must reject these arguments.

3. Arguments against

A. Physical Determinism
Everything in nature has an exact cause and obeys the laws of physics, chemistry, biology. If I bump into a thing, the collision follows the laws of motion. In raising my hand I obey the energetics of muscle and nerve transmission. Even though the laws of science are not fully understood, whatever they are, they are such, and they take no holidays. A man walking down the street is as subservient to physics as a man in orbit about the earth. True, we ourselves are part of the equation but no one has shown that willing itself adds anything to the force/energy of a body. Which dyne or erg can be credited to volition? Whether or no someone falls voluntarily, he falls by the same laws of physics.

Again, as scientific laws control our actions, they also control our being acted upon. If we are cold we shiver. If rain falls on us we are bothered. If the air is too polluted we can hardly breathe and are in a bad mood. Physical causes impinging on us, change us and cause us to want and to feel in certain ways. If we try to change the course of these causes we do so by calling on other physical causes to counter them (e.g. I try to get warm).

This is the gist of many such arguments for physical determinism. Let us look at two such in more detail:

a. Calculability
Laplace tried to draw a determinist conclusion from Newtonian physics.[4] If the speed, direction, etc. of a set of objects and the forces acting on them at one moment are completely known, then the speed, direction, etc. of these objects can be completely speci-

fied at any later time. We can, for instance, predict where the planets will be a month from now, because we know their present positions, velocities, etc. and the forces on them. Thus their future state is completely determined. Consider, for simplicity, three billiard balls on a pool table. If the speed, forces etc. are known at time t=0 sec., then we can determine the same quantities at any other time t. This is the way of mathematical physics. We should know the mass, density, shape, angular momentum, center of gravity, coefficients of elasticity, friction, etc.

In practice this gets complicated very quickly, but never mind—the point remains the same: full knowledge of the present situation gives full knowledge of the future situation, so whether we actually figure it all out or not, the present situation determines the future situation.

This limited paradigm is then expanded to cover all motions and all situations including that human future which we may think subject to deliberation and choice. So chance and choice are equally illusory.

How to counter this? One defense of freedom is based on the quantum theory. Quantum physics claims that within limits set by the Heisenberg Uncertainty Principle, there are real indeterminacies in matter (ontological interpretation) or theoretical limits to any possible knowledge of the position and momentum of a body (epistemological interpretation).[5]

We leave this counter-argument aside because 1) the theory is very complex, 2) its scale seems too tiny to effect anything on the human level, and 3) it leaves us at the mercy of the 'physics of the moment'. If quantum theory itself is supplanted at a more fundamental level, must we reargue this?

Instead let's analyze how we arrive at the view of nature as like billiard balls. We set aside all idiosyncratic properties of things and consider them as material points of some sort, as 'masses in motion'. Having stripped away everything else, we can analyze these bodies in the way physics does. This is a very proper and successful way to go about physics. To put a man on the moon exactly such a procedure was followed. The sense of humor or moral character of the astronaut was not considered in calculating the precise forces and velocities to land him on the moon.

Exactly. And that is why the argument doesn't convince.

If we know where the planets are at 10 PM we can predict where they will be at 11 PM. But given the location and speed of nine friends at a party at 10 PM we cannot predict where they will be at 11 PM.

We get to view bodies as physics does by 'abstracting down' - removing all but those properties relevant to physics. But then to believe that what is left, is all that truly exists, is to fool ourselves. After all, it was we who removed all the other features. If we forget how we got there, we misphilosophize.

The laws of physics describe us because we are masses in motion. But that's not all we are. The astronaut's sense of humor is not considered when finding the forces to put him in orbit. But that doesn't mean he has no sense of humor. The laws of physics describe billiard balls more exhaustively than they do humans because billiard balls are more nearly just masses in motion.

b. Force/Energy

This argument looks not at the calculability but at the forces/energies themselves. Physical forces control action. Willing does not add any physical force. Therefore, talk about free will should be cut short, it contributes nothing.

Although we hear stories where 'will power' contributes a great force and though many doctors believe will power is a big help in getting well, this power has not been quantified. So it is better to counter this argument some other way.

Free will could be thought of as either the initiator of forces or the specifier of which forces will be initiated. It may take the same force to reach for a peach as for a plum, so something other than force determines which you do. Free will could control forces without itself being a force -much as a coach determines who goes in and out of a basketball game without himself being one of the players.

There is a theorem in physics/chemistry: In any reaction or change the total energy before equals the total energy after. Energy is neither created nor destroyed, it merely changes form. If so, what role is left for human free will?

Free will specifies energy. The fact that I have a fixed amount of money doesn't tell whether I will buy plates or skates. The conservation law requires that what I take from one account, I put in another. But it doesn't specify or forbid any transaction! If I shake a man's hand or refuse to do so, energy is conserved precisely. But will I shake his hand?

Finally, the initiation of motion is mysterious. Does an annoying breeze move me or merely motivate me to move?

Two cases when free will seems to 'stick out' are when I try to resist an impulse or when I try to do something but cannot because of a physical impairment. Normally wanting to raise my arm and doing it are so joined that I am unaware of any separate act of volition coming before the arm is raised. But if the arm is impeded by injury, my "will sticks out". Paradoxically, here, free will is most prominent when physical causation is most overwhelming.

B. Psychological Determinism
Odors bring back memories, a shower lifts morale, bells are sweet or sad. Physical causes overlap psychological ones. A change of food or air can take us from being deflated to being fresh, crisp, in-focus. Here we consider two other types of more purely psychological determiners -those we are unaware of and those we are aware of.

a. Non-conscious
Freud claims that subconscious forces determine our behavior.[6] A host of subsurface vectors–complexes, memories, associations, fears–act on us to determine our subsequent life. Early childhood vectors are especially formative. This host of subliminal forces is itself rooted in instincts of survival and sexuality and plays itself out through the creation and interaction of Superego, Ego and Id– the three components of human personality.

Psychoanalysis, by diving beneath the surface, brings these vectors to awareness. In this way the patient can lead a more balanced, less neurotic life. Freed up from the control of dark and unknown forces, the patient becomes more sovereign, more serene, happier.

Two difficulties leap out:
1) If we are captive to subconscious forces before we know of

them, how will mere knowledge of them get us anywhere? Consciousness and knowledge are not in the drivers seat, instincts and the subconscious are. Isn't this almost like hoping that knowledge of death will avert it? And if more knowledge means more autonomy and freedom, then doesn't some knowledge (of the sort we presumably already have) mean some freedom?

2) If all is determined by the subconscious, the Freudian theory itself is a subrational product. But it appears to be the fruit of some conscious intellecting. This is a self-referential contradiction: The very speaking or even thinking of the theory contradicts its own content. And why talk to us, if we are incapable of rationally weighing his theory?

Apart from whether Freud's analysis of subconscious forces is true, a modified Freudianism could at least avoid contradiction. Subconscious forces may play a huge role in our desires, aversions and actions without controlling us completely. Knowledge of these forces may be liberating, if increased awareness means increased sovereignty -which is one kind of freedom. Knowledge of why we feel a certain way helps us step over these feelings if we deeply care to. If I realize why I have a fierce dislike of someone (he reminds me of something troubling), I can try to rise above my feeling. This enhances my freedom.

b. Conscious

Could we be determined by conscious factors? Hardly, if we are directly aware of our freedom. But let's leave that aside. Someone may say we are deluding ourselves.

There is a theory which we call "determinism of the apparent better". It appears to be held by the medieval thinker Godfrey of Fontaines and perhaps by others.[7] The traditional explanation might begin as follows:

There are in us two components or faculties: that which apprehends, judges, understands reality -intellect; that which desires or wants -will. It is very different to think "this is water" and "I want to drink water now". All presentings including judgments about the goodness of something are up to the intellect. Intellect apprehends, considers, doubts, reflects, compares. Will only desires, chooses, loves, hates, takes a stand.

We can simplify the theory by reducing all situations of choice to a choice of pairs or a series of pairs. Either x or not-x. Either x or y. Either a drink or no drink. Either I go or I don't go. Either I go to Rwanda or to Burundi. Intellect presents to the agent or to the agent's will such a pair including information about which looks better. The eye of this theory is that the will must choose what appears better. 'What appears better' is itself dependent on what kind of person you are at the moment. And what-kind-of- person-you-are may depend on past choices, but it is not a free principle in the present choice.

Suppose you have two slabs of butter and you find one rancid, one fresh. The judgment 'this butter is rancid' is not volitional, it is just a gustatory or an olfactory fact. Possessing a normal constitution, can you prefer rancid butter?

Once we set up all choices in pairs, like a scale which must bend to the side with the greater weight, the will must incline to the side with the greater (apparent) goodness.

[A philosophical experiment to show that it is the apparent better that controls choice is Buridan's Ass. The animal is faced with two identical bales of hay symmetrically placed. It starves to death because neither is an apparent better and so the will cannot be moved to choose. Opponents would say the example cuts the other way. The animal would eat something, thereby proving that will is an active power, and leaving the burden with other philosophers.]

The strength of the theory is this: What else would you say? Given the choice between a free $100,000 and $100 who would choose the $100? And why? [There might be a 'why' -if I take the $100,000 my name will be in the paper and I will have to hire a guard to protect me. But then that is a fact to put in the balance.]

But if everything is already put in the balance how then can one choose the lesser? If there is no 'why' (I choose the known worse just because or really becauselessly), then in defending freedom are we defending spontaneity or absurdity? Is free will to be vindicated only by absurd actions?

What about this theory? It leaves freedom-as-mastery alone, but not free choice. Actions are truly one's own. A brave person makes the brave choice, a sensitive person is sensitive. Choosing otherwise however, is quite impossible.

It also allows praise or blame, but in a funny sense. If a man stops by the road to give me a lift, I can thank him (or God) for his being the kind of person he is, but I must realize he could not have done otherwise! Doesn't this sound strange?

Also, the experience of regret weighs against conscious determinism. On Tuesday I regret a deed done on Monday. I am very clear and very sorry that I made a wrong choice -not because of a mistake, not because of the harm I didn't count on, etc., but simply because I know what I did was wrong. Godfrey might say this can occur because now I am a new person (I feel safe, I've sobered up, etc.) and so I see the past choice differently. But is that what regretters say? Do they regret having been a certain type of person, or do they regret a certain choice given the person they were and the possibilities truly open to them then? Is this experience of regret an illusion or is possible to choose otherwise?

The "theory of the apparent better" brings to mind several topics interesting on their own. Let us look at them as a digression–without trying to force any connections.

Three come to mind:
  i) reform of self
  ii) dialectic of intellect/will
  iii) special case of 'highly automatic virtue'

i) reform of self. The addict is a good example. Because someone is addicted, a drug is the apparent better. Can he reform? According to the above theory, he cannot do so by any simple act of the will. As long as his body chemistry is such and such, the drug will seem the better choice, and as long as it seems the better choice, he will choose it. But something external could change his body chemistry, and once that was changed, the drug would no longer seem the better and so would not be chosen. If (at a time when not faced with the drug choice) the addict made some other choice (e.g. to fly to where there would be no such drug available for six months) he could bring about a change in what seems better to him. This is close to the model used for alcoholics. The alcoholic is deflected from his choice-pattern by bringing external factors to bear which will then help him choose differently because he will be different. A final example–A famous 20th century comic writer went to commit suicide by drowning. But he was stung by a jellyfish. So instead

he lived for several decades, converted to Catholicism, wrote many comic novels. Presumably the jellyfish sting hurt, this angered or upset him, this changed his overall mood, in the new mood suicide no longer seemed the 'apparent better'. This sequence is probable, though the whole episode sounds like something out his own novels.
ii) dialectic of intellect/will. a) You have to care about a thing to pay attention to it. b) You have to pay attention to a thing to know about it. c) You have to know a little about a thing to care about it. Isn't this a circle? A virtuous (non-vicious) circle perhaps, but still a circle. So how do we get started?

If I want to go to Hawaii it's because I've heard of its fantastic climate or waves or I have friends there. If I never heard of Hawaii, can I want to go there? But to come to learn about a subject seems to require having a certain affinity for it. To learn organic chemistry you have to want to learn it. But how can you want to learn it, if you don't have an inkling of what it is? How to start?

One model relates knowing to loving as follows:[8] Each of us has an intellect (power of apprehension, understanding, etc.) and a will (power of appetition, desiring, loving). [They have to be different powers because we don't love everything we know.]

The intellect presents a thing to the will to decide on. A kid is at a fair. His intellect presents 'what it is like to ride an elephant' together with 'I have enough money with me to pay for it'. The will then says yes or no. But the kid may be afraid that the elephant will be too big or the trainer won't come along. So he investigates, but he wouldn't if he weren't interested. That is, the will tells the intellect to find out.

Intellect tells will which is better (specification), but will tells intellect to pay attention (consideration, exercise). The will flips on the light and then the intellect tells the will about the furniture and the pictures in the room. The will then is pleased, or if not, goes to another room and turns on the lights there. [Will and intellect, of course, are not separate from the agent.]

This is expressed as:

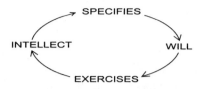

This too is a circle! What gets the ball rolling? Aquinas posits God as the first mover of intellect/will to untangle this 'dialectic'.

iii) special case of 'highly automatic virtue'

"No se cerraron sus ojos quando vió las cuernas cerca,"

[His eyes did not close when he saw the horns near,]

Frederico Garcia Lorca wrote that high praise for his matador friend in "Lament for Ignacio Sanchez Mejias".[9] What are we to make of `ingrained virtue'? For Aristotle, virtues are habits.[10] The more deeply habitual the generosity, courage, truthfulness- the more excellent the person. The matador's bravery percolates to his very eyelids! For Kant,[11] on the other hand, the more a deed proceeds from an act of pure good will, the more virtuous it is. And what could be purer than deeds which go against the grain, against one's feeling or inclination? A brave deed is to be praised more if done by a timorous man full of trembling and very aware of preferring to be somewhere else.

Who's right? Aristotle and Kant come from very different principles. Could this be a resolution?: Ingrained habits of generosity, courage, etc. are indeed a mark of greatness. Automatic courage is the mark of a most brave man. But the courageous act of a timorous man is the more courageous deed. Aristotle's man, Kant's deed. But many deeds make a new man and by a congealed capital of volition the once timorous man becomes brave.

To summarize:

Against subconscious determinism it is argued that the conscious intellectual elaboration of the theory refutes the theory itself (it self destructs) and the practice of psychoanalysis also labors against the theory.

On conscious determinism we highlight these points. It does not oppose all freedom; it leaves open the question of what focuses attention in the first place; it allows us to praise/blame good and evil individuals because it allows mastery freedom.

And the theory has problems of its own. It may be yoked to a certain mechanics of mind. Regret or gladness over past choice seems to point to free choice. Finally, if we have inner experience of free choice, the theory is undermined.

C. Theological Determinism
These deep arguments occur only if a certain sense of God is kept in mind. However, this sort of God is what the main currents of monotheistic religion do hold. The arguments are also important to some who take them elsewhere. Lucretius teaches that the gods have no providence for man and that this is good news, even medicine, because it removes all fear of the beyond.[12] John Calvin claims that some are doomed by God to go to hell no matter what they do - predestination.[13] In the 17th century, topics of grace and predestination were the rage in salons and drawing rooms all over Europe.

a. Causality
God is the cause of everything other than Himself. So God is the cause of all human action as well. For if we were to do anything that was not caused by God, we would be the first cause of some line of being or action. There would be in the world of things and events, some reality that was not created by God. Since this contradicts our first statement, we must be simply carrying out the program God has put in us. Any notion of free will is an illusion. [This issue is even more acute if evil action is involved.]

b. Knowledge
God knows everything. Since he cannot err, what he knows must come to pass. I may be in a great dither about whether to buy a blue or a green car next week. But God knows I will choose the blue one and since He cannot be wrong, I will choose the blue one. I may feel free but it is already decided, since God cannot be mistaken.

These arguments attack all three senses of freedom. We summarize briefly responses given to neutralize or weaken these objections and leave open the space for freedom.

i) There are secondary causes. God sometimes chooses to act through other instruments. He chooses some agents to carry out His will in a fixed and determined manner like robots or tools. He chooses others to carry out his will in their own proper mode. Humans carry out His will as conscious free agents not as stones or rivers or planets do.

No human examples are adequate, but let me try one to get a partial glimpse of how one 'tool' can put more of itself in its action than another. A painter's brush is a secondary cause of the painting. But the brush puts little of itself into the painting. It could have as easily served a very different painting. A singer's voice is a 'freer' secondary cause. Her song is plaintive or jealous. Perhaps it could not so easily bear another anthem. The emotion is not only in her heart or intention, but in her voice as well. So by analogy:

voice : brush :: our causality : stone's causality

On evil: sin and evil are actually non-being. If we use our free agency as God directs us, we put that being into the world which God puts –like the voice and the singer. However, if we sin, we do not become first efficient causes of a line of being uncaused by God. Instead we become first deficient causes of a line of non-being which is non-willed by God.

ii) Against God's omniscient foreknowledge, freedom is defended by the claim that God is outside of time. For him everything is present in one full instant -the standing now. So God doesn't foreknow, he simply knows. Is it as if He knows (our time) that I will buy the blue car at the instant that I choose it?

Not all theists would make the same counter arguments. Do these suggestions solve the problems? It would be arrogant to brush things aside so quickly. A caution: what do we know about divine understanding and volition? But if freedom and causality are not inherently contradictory, they can be reconciled somehow. If they are inherently contradictory, there will be problems even if God is not considered. To delve deeper into these questions would take us far from introductory philosophy.

IV. Footnotes and References

1. Thomas Aquinas, *Summa Theologica I*, q82 a2.
2. Sartre, John Paul, *Being and Nothingness* and *"Cartesian Freedom"*.

3. Duns Scotus, *God and Creatures, The Quodlibetal Questions*, (tr. Felix Allantis and Allan Wolter), Princeton University Press, 1975, q.17. See also the article in the Encyclopedia of Philosophy (under Duns) by Allan Wolter, vol. 2, p.427-436 and his article *"Native Freedom of the Will as a Key to the Ethics of Scotus,"* Studia Scholastica-Scotistica 5 Rome 1972, p.359-370

4. Laplace, Pierre Simon de, *Philosophical Essays on Probabilities,* (tr. by F.W. Truscott and F.L. Emory), Dover, New York, 1951, p.4.

5. Heisenberg, Werner, *Physics and Philosophy*, Harper and Brothers, New York, 1958.

6. These ideas permeate his work. See e.g., *A General Introduction to Psycho-Analysis*, p.486 (Great Books, vol.54). Also see *Beyond the Pleasure Principle* and *The Ego and the Id* in the same volume.

7. Godfrey of Fontaines, *Quodlibetal Questions* (in Les Philosophes Belges, Louvain, Belgium published between 1904 and 1937 tomes 2,3,4,5 and 14). Some key questions are Quodlibet 6, question 6 (Q6q6), Q6q7, Q10q14, Q15q6.

8. Thomas Aquinas, *Summa Theologica I*, q82 a4, q83.

9. Lorca, Frederico Garcia *Llanto por Ignacio Sánchez Mejías*, part 2, lines 42-43.

10. Aristotle, Nichomachean Ethics, Book II etc.

11. Kant, Immanuel, *Foundations of the Metaphysics of Morals,* (tr. Lewis Beck), Bobbs-Merrill, Indianapolis, 1959, p.16 and elsewhere.

12. Lucretius, *De Rerum Natura,* Book I, lines 46-50, 150-158, 934-950.

13. Calvin, John, *Institutes of the Christian Religion*, (tr. Ford Lewis Battles), The Library of Christian Classics, vol. 21, The Westminster Press, 1973, Book III, ch.23,1-3, p.947-951.

Other sources are too numerous to mention. Freedom is of special interest to theologians. See St. Augustine's *On Free Choice of the Will* for an early and important discussion.

And it is of great interest to psychology, but we do not try to develop the literature on this.

Finally "external" freedom is of great concern to political philosophy.

V. Questions

External

1) What is the difference between freedom for something and freedom from something?

2) Is external freedom always increased if more choices are made available or if one's knowledge increases?

3) Democracy and freedom are commonly joined as if fully compatible. But they are very different and can even be opposed at times. Does democracy maximize freedom compared to e.g., anarchy? What is the best political set up for external freedom?

4) Should government maximize freedom? What are some freedoms government (or something else) should restrict? Why?

Internal

5) Most challenges to free will come from causality. But are the notions themselves opposed? Is the idea of something freely causing a contradictory idea? Give definitions of both and compare carefully.

6) What is the relation between intellect and freedom? Could there be intellectual beings without free will? Could unintelligent beings have free will?

7) Some claim experience or direct awareness of free will, others pass this by. Are their experiences different? Comment. What are we to make of this?

8) Is free will itself a good? Is it intrinsically better to have it than not to? Elaborate.

9) Find a psychologist who is not a determinist. Investigate his/her views on motivation, fulfillment, etc.

10) Some oppose freedom to happiness -saying we would be happier unfree. Comment.

11) Explain in your own words one argument made above.

12) Give any other arguments pro/con free will and any other refutations to these arguments.

TOOLS

One way to do philosophy is to think it all out originally for oneself. This can be strong, timely and fresh. Abelard came to a view on universals not unlike that of Aristotle, without knowing Aristotle's view. Another way to do philosophy is to make one's own the true thought that has come before -the "shoulders of giants" approach. This can have its drawbacks: One may repeat past mistakes, thought-lessly follow ideas without plumbing their depths, reuse formulas that have lost all meaning or apply elsewhere. But it can have great advantages: By absorbing some of the true thought of others one is freed from the prejudices and thought molds of one's own time/ place. The mindscapes of others add dimension and color, push back horizons. There's a huge saving of mental energy. Also it puts us square in the middle of a great community -"truthers" from every-where and everywhen.

Insights and distinctions come from all over. A deep and clear well of fundamental distinctions is Aristotle.[1] Another rich source is Frege, Husserl, Heidegger, and the philosophy of language in recent times.[2]

While 100% agreement in philosophy is not to be had (e.g., some philosophers say everything is material and George Berkeley denies the existence of matter) -logical tools are generally agreed upon.

The metaphysical tools are another matter. Disagreement is most keen. We let them stand on their own. But we do flag by author those views that may be peculiar to a philosopher.

Logical Tools

Self Reference

"This sentence has seven words"
There is something wrong with the above sentence. It is false. But notice the way its false. We tell it is false not by looking at what the

sentence is about -there is nothing implausable about seven word sentences- but at the sentence itself. This way of reflecting back on a statement itself is called self-reference.

First a few more examples: "This sentence has five words" is self-referentially true. "This sentence is in German" is self-referentially false. "Peaches are blue", "You have a Saint Bernard", "There are eleven liquid elephants in Liechtenstein" are true or false, not self- referentially, but depending on whether they correspond to real or even possible facts. To find if "Mars has two moons" is true, you look at the sky not the sentence.

"Cretans always lie" cannot be true if uttered by a Cretan. Are there things which, even if they could be true, are unutterable? Does cynicism lead to silence?

Is self-reference a trick or semi-comical move? Quite the contrary, it has powerful repercussions for whole philosophies as we shall see. But there is a serious problem with self-reference itself. Bertrand Russell discovered a contradiction in set theory if all kinds of self-reference and sets are allowed. [3]

A popularization of the problem is this: There is a village in which the barber shaves all and only those who do not shave themselves. Does the barber shave himself? If he does, then he doesn't. If he doesn't, then he does. The easy way out is to say there is no such village or the barber lives elsewhere. In other cases it's not so easy. A set is a collection of most any kind. Some sets do not include themselves. The set of all tea cups is not a tea cup, it's a set. Russell's considers a special set: X = the set of all sets that do not include themselves. Does X belong to X? If it doesn't, then it does. If it does, then it doesn't.

He suggests a way out. Layer all statements in such a way as to avoid self-reference. Individual things like an okapi, a camel, Ethelred the Unready, Heloise, Ted Williams and are in class zero (C_0). Statements about them are in class one (C_1). Statements about these are in class two (C_2), and so on. His commandment is: Don't mix classes or categories! Self-referential problems are avoided if you forbid mixing categories.

"Ann has three letters" is a pun that involves mixing categories -the girl Ann (C_0) and the word Ann (C_1).*

A statement-about-a-camel is not a camel so we can clearly separate them. If you said "Camels are unkind" to a camelophile and I later criticized your remark as unkind, I am making a C_2 statement that your C_1 statement was unkind. I am not saying or implying anything about the kindness of camels because my 'unkind' refers to C_1, not C_0 reality.

Russell's solution is ingenious but it throws out too much. The word 'camel' is not a camel, but the word 'word' is a word. A statement about statements is a statement. Awareness of awareness is awareness.

Reflection is a kind of doubling back. We think about what we are doing. We also think about thinking. To outlaw self-reference it seems you have to outlaw reflection. [Why do some people ignore reflection? Is it because you have to reflect to realize there is reflection?]

People miss self-reference. "I am using only sentences with ten words." might be said by someone pointing to a paper on which he was writing such a poem. He is "thinking away" from his own utterance and does not notice any inconsistency.

A massive dose of self-referential inconsistency occurs in the speculations of David Hume.[4] In *A Treatise of Human Nature*, Hume denies the existence of self, real causes, subjects, objects, extensions in time, etc. But if none such exist, how can a man, David Hume, write a connected piece of reasoning about human nature, to be read by us now, as it was written by him then, etc.! The arguments self-destruct in the way 'This sentence is in German.' does.

The self-referential challenge can be thrown at any theory that says: ideas are totally the products of the era, economic conditions or psychology of their originators.

Karl Marx says in the *Communist Manifesto*, "The charges against Communism made from a religious, a philosophical, and generally, from an ideological standpoint, are not deserving of serious examination. Does it require deep intuition to comprehend that a man's ideas, views, and conceptions, in a word, man's consciousness, changes with every change in the condition of his material existence, in his social relations and in his social life?"[5]

If so, then this idea itself is but a product of Marx' own consciousness which itself is but a product of 19th century industrialism. How silly to say!: It is timelessly true that all ideas are time bound.

Many could save themselves from such embarassingly easy refutation by toning down their polemic. Marx could show how much our outlook, feelings and judgments are shaped or shaded by the reality of our everyday workworld. This would be a rich contribution that leaves room for timeless truths.

One more example: Karl Popper claims that statements are one of these three: (empirically) falsifiable or meaningless or tautologies (e.g. six is a half dozen).[6] Call this claim Q. No one thinks Q itself is meaningless or a tautology. This leaves only the first choice. But what experiment would falsify Q. It doesn't appear to be an empirical claim at all. Then on its own terms (i.e., self-referentially), Q is false. Argued another way -to be true, Q must be falsifiable! And if it is not falsifiable, it is false. Strange talk!

Popper's claim self-destructs.

Self-reference is a powerful tool even though there are complex problems involving it. Self-cancelling statements [I am asleep.] are comical and philosophy itself seems comical or freakish in its concern for self-reference. Philosophy looks at other things and at itself, at its own looking.

When Frege heard of Russell's contradiction, he feared the foundations of arithmetic were crumbling. Perhaps the contradiction can be avoided by restricting what counts as a set. Our set X above may not be sufficiently well staked out to qualify as a set. This is tough ground. Fine minds have mined it. Some such solution is better than the rejection of reflection -including the very excellent reflection that led Russell to his discovery in the first place.

*Perhaps here is a good place to scratch in a little language philosophy. We *use* the word Ann to designate a person and *mention* the word Ann to designate the name itself. But things can get more complex. The word brady means slow (in Greek and medicine), not a person so named. But the word brady itself is not slow (the word polysyllabic itself is polysyllabic). Contrast this with "Paul is little". The word paul itself is little (four letters) and the person was once little, and the word means little (though not in English). But if we move to Chinese–*xiao* is a name, it means little and the word itself is little (only four letters {although not in Chinese characters}). In these cases we have at least three items: meaning, mention and use of a word. These examples bring on the question: What language are we in? It does matter. "Weiss is white" is hardly identical to "Weiss is weiss", even though weiss means white in German. If we use English to teach Irish, Irish is the language, English is the metalanguage. More generally what sign system are we in? Can we be in more than one? E.g., can we be in a written and spoken system at the same time? A sign is the unity of signifier (what indicates) and signified (what is indicated). Considering a language to be a sign system, even within a given language things can shift around: 1) A sign can be a signifier. An ad for an expensive liquor has an opulent setting which itself promises wealth and ease. 2) A sign can be a signified. I quote a speech without meaning it myself. "Neither a borrower, nor a lender be."–Shakespeare doesn't preach that, Polonius does. 3) A signifier can be a sign. An affected accent is a sign on its own of snobbery, apart from what is said with the accent. 4) A signifier can be a signified. In our example above, `Ann' has been shifted over to become the object designated.

"Shift" is a key notion here. We shift from one system to another when we quote, change point of view or language, disengage assent. We need not take this as a linguistic cul- de-sac or quagmire. Rejoice (read Joyce)! -this is what makes *Finnegans Wake* possible. Philosophy thinks playfully so it plays with language. It may need to do so to have its say.

Yet it is sophistry to hide in a fog of our own making. Two important limits come to mind: i) We can quote without agreeing with what we quote, but we cannot step back so far that we discredit all our own speech as if inside some endless metaquote. To do so would be to allow "I am silent". ii) We cannot close off self-referential challenges. "Levi- Strauss says what Borero Indians are doing when they say they are parakeets -but what is Levi-Strauss doing when he says this." [7] To reject this kind of question is to undermine any universal science. Our science then slides toward ideology or idiosyncracy, prejudice or point-of-view. Everybody grants that parts of science do well on parts of reality. But if there is to be a science of the whole, it must include an account of itself, of its own activity, of "sciencing".

Proof/Evidence

A proof has three parts: 1) what you start with - the premises 2) what you end up with -the conclusion and 3) the logic -or the connections. To be a good argument the premises must be true and the logic must be correct. Logical errors can be detected and labeled. The main thing is to get true premises. No argument can be stronger than its weakest premise.

Where do premises come from? Well, they might come from other arguments. But they can't all come that way–that leads to an infinite run-around. There must be some premises that don't come from other arguments. Underived, they must be self-evident. When you understand what they mean and think about them, you see they are true. The bad news–some things can't be proven. We must get back to unproven premises.

The good news–not everything needs to be proven. If a premise is self-evident it is silly to try to prove it. Some arguers insistently demand proof of everything. This shows ignorance of the nature of proof. The project to prove everything demands that there be no 'starters', no self-evident premises. Thus, actually nothing can be proven.

Some starting principles involve little more than a comparison of ideas: A mother is older than her daughter. The whole is greater than any proper part.

Few arguments get off the ground using only such simple principles. Euclid's geometry was considered the model for this kind of pure reasoning. A small set of underived notions (point, line, etc.) are coupled with a group of self-evident axioms. From this is spun out a bevy of theorems and corollaries until a whole book of geometry is in one's hand. (Without going deep into problems of knowledge and certitude) we can use common sense and experience to supply us with plenty of premises. E.g., Some animals are more dangerous than others. Nobody wants to stop being happy. Plants can't talk. Rocks don't have a sense of humor.

Common sense can be tricky because it may be mere common opinion or even common prejudice or just a stylish stance. Absolute universal statements are hard to be certain about. One counter-example undermines them. What if we found a talking plant? Should we worry that this might happen?

In any case, most of the time we have to settle for propositions that are less than absolutely certain. And since a proof is only as certain as its weakest premise, ironclad proofs are hard to come by. Items that favor a statement being true are evidence. Evidence is of many sorts. Evidence in chemistry is not the same as evidence in human affairs. We feel confident in saying "Acids react with bases." even if we have tested only 15 cases. But if we find 15 overweight murderers, we don't conclude "Murderers are pinguid.". How much evidence is enough? Take our claim "Rocks don't have a sense of humor.". How much evidence do we require before we are willing to assent to this? As detectives or scientists we pile up evidence to back up our theories. These are often about inaccessible things. They may involve events that are over and done with, hidden, unrepeatable–the motives of those who killed Caesar. Or they may be about unobservables like quarks. Evidence is piled up linking cigarette smoking and cancer. Is the link circumstantial? causal? certain?

Some truths throw themselves at us without our asking. Others resist the fiercest investigation!

Order of Discovery/Order of Being

The order in which we find out about things is not usually the order in which they come about. For instance, we discover a dead man and reason back to find who shot him. But the shot is prior to the death. We feel the earthquake, but not the tectonic plates moving. We see the clouds but not the evaporation and condensation that formed them. We find effects and reason back to causes. This is the common order of discovery. In logic, reasoning from effects to causes is called *a posteriori*. In reality things proceed from cause to effect. This is the order of being. The murder came before the discovery of the body. In logic, reasoning from causes to effects is called *a priori*. Normally, we think that a given cause always has the same effect. If a cloud gets a certain charge, lightning results. If water drops to a certain temperature, freezing results. An exception: If a cause acts freely, you cannot always tell the effect from knowledge of the cause. You may know Mavourneen well, but you can't predict what she will do.

A priori reasoning is similar to deductive reasoning in logic. If p stands for certain atmospheric conditions and q stands for rain, then we can reason as follows:

$$p{\longrightarrow}q, p, \text{ therefore } q.$$

The relation between theories and observations is logically similar to that holding between causes and effects. If a given theory is true, then, in a given situation, it should yield a definite predictable observation.

However, reasoning from effects or observations is very different. A doctor is faced with certain symptoms. He tries to find the cause. But two different diseases may show the same symptoms. Generally more than one cause can give the same effect, more than one theory explain the same facts.

Suppose a given theory or cause p, calls for a certain observable effect q. Suppose we do find q. Then we have:

$$p{\longrightarrow}q, q$$

But (r,s,t) could also cause q, so nothing can be concluded.

However, if we do not find q, when the theory implies we should, we have:

$$p{\longrightarrow}q, \text{ not } q, \text{ therefore not } p \quad \text{which is valid.}$$

So we can disprove theories or reject causes a lot more easily than we can prove them! This is the basis of Popper's claim that worthwhile propositions are only falsifiable, never verifiable. [See our Self-reference]

But is it true that a theory can be falsified this simply? Pierre Duhem claims that an experiment involves a whole constellation of background understandings. [8] If something goes wrong, it may not be the theory itself, but one of the background notions, that is at fault.

Take the experiments to show that living things can only come from other living things. Did a negative result (living things found in a flask where the theory presumed they could not be) disprove the theory? No, instead a background assumption was changed -microbes might be carried in the air and fall into the flask.

Duhem concludes that we cannot falsify a theory in a single experiment. Again, we suspect he goes too far.

Another distinction is between a 'fact' and a 'reasoned fact'. We know people of a certain group are more susceptible to a disease (fact). But we do not know why (reasoned fact). The former is like an effect, the latter like a cause. We don't have to know the reason before we accept the fact.

Sense/Reference

Gottlob Frege distinguishes between sense (*Sinn*) and reference (*Bedeutung*).[9] The sense of a proposition is what it means. The reference is what it is about. The referent is the object the proposition points to.

These seem to be the same -what a sentence means and the thing it is about. But Frege shows they are not. His example is the Morning Star and the Evening Star. The last bright star sometimes seen in the East before sunrise is called the Morning Star. The first bright star seen in the West after sunset is the Evening Star. Now it turns out that both these 'stars' are the planet Venus.

We have two different meanings but one object referred to. So sense and reference must be different. Another way to argue this: If both had the same meaning then "The Morning Star is the Evening Star" would be a tautology like "A is A" and obvious to everyone. In fact, it took much effort to find that both are Venus.

Not every sense has a real object that it points to. "The present king of France is bald." is an intelligible utterance, it is not gibberish. But it has no referent since, in France, the subject (and subjects!) don't exist.

In the discussion of happiness by Aristotle, it is agreed that happiness is what we want. It is a final purpose, desirable for itself, not for something else, etc. We agree on a sense. But what content does happiness have? What fills the bill? What is the referent?

This distinction brings to mind others -e.g., between the empty and the full, etc. in such as Husserl and Marcel.

Univocal/Equivocal/Analogical

A word used in one and the same sense is univocal. An oak tree and a maple tree are both trees in the same sense of the word. A

Logic

word used in unrelated or totally different senses is equivocal. A savings bank and the bank of a river are equivocal uses of the word bank.

If a word is used in ways that are somewhat the same and somewhat different, then its use is analogical.

Univocal and equivocal are the easy ones. Logic requires univocal use. All X is Y. All Y is Z. Therefore, all X is Z. For this to work, each term must be univocal. Equivocal uses lead to equivocations. Riddles or puns thrive on equivocal usages. The different senses are usually easy to discern. Analogy is the big one. If there were no such thing, philosophy would be much clearer. Words (and the things and kinds they describe?) would be either identically the same or totally different. Reality doesn't go that way. Analogical uses are many. "The discussion generated more heat than light." uses three words in a figurative sense. Can we totally separate the metaphorical use of light from its physical meaning?

Let us look at a few kinds of analogy.

In mathematics, analogy is ratio. a:b::c:d or a/b=c/d.Biology speaks of the analogy of function and the analogy of form. The trunk of an elephant is analogous to the hand in function, but to the upper lip in form. Simile and metaphor are based on analogy. Metonomy or "transferred naming" is also. We speak of the mouth of a river or of a cave, a head of state or of lettuce, the heart of an apple, the apple of my eye. Someone called the sun the "day's eye"; someone else saw the daisy as the sun.

Some analogies are all pervasive. The analogy between seeing or light and intellectual or spiritual awareness is everywhere -in Plato, Aristotle, the Gospels, the Gnostics.

Linguistics speaks of false analogy as a force making new forms: [sing:sang::bring:brang]. Cheeseburger is formed from hamburger as if hamburgers were made of ham or there were a city on the Elbe called Cheeseburg!

Can we make a table of all classes of analogy? Analogies are between a thing and its effects, its sign, its cause, a part of it, a use of it, something with a similar shape, something that reminds us of it, etc. Our list might go on and on, the playfulness of mind and language is great. If analogy were limited to linguistics or mathematics, it would not be so central to philosophy. But for some thinkers the core notions of philosophy (being, life, beauty, good, etc.) are analogical.

Aristotle gives special attention to the analogy where several meanings link to one central sense. Fruits are healthy (as a cause), a complexion is healthy (as a sign) but a person is healthy in the primary sense that health inheres in him. For Aristotle, "is" is analogical. It can be said of substances, properties of substance, potential rather than actual being and even of privations. We say: There is a horse. The horse is brown. An acorn is an oak. There is no unicorn. Entity or substance is in the primary sense.

If everything were equally real, we should perhaps get new words to go around analogy completely. But if there are depths in reality, analogy is ubiquitous. A moss is alive, but is it alive in the same sense as a human? Aquinas says analogical language is the proper way to speak of God. We take a notion like "wise", strip it of all imperfection and limitation and apply it pre-eminently and analogously to God. For him, this steers between agnosticism (equivocal predication) and anthropomorphism (univocal predication).

Taking uncreated being as being in the primary sense, he applies the analogy of "is" to God. God is, all other things "have" their being. Indeed, "is" or "to be" is the best name for God.

In the Allegory of the Cave, Plato [10] tells of captives chained so the only thing they can see are shadows of images reflected by firelight against a wall. The prisoners are "like to us" [Republic 514]. To speak of what is more real than we are and of what is most real, he looks at lower worlds and sets up an analogy of at least six layers. A:B::B:C::C:D::D:E::E:F. A = the supreme good, B = the intelligible, eidetic world, C = us, D = physical things, E = images and artificial objects, F = shadows.

Analogy, far from being a linguistic curse, is a tool for gripping things that are very slippery–like and unlike.

Some Fallacies

Fallacies cannot be perfectly precise. Some fallacies are not fallacious 100% of the time -it depends on what is being argued. For instance, 'an appeal to the people' is a fallacy if you use it to claim a mathematical statement is true, but not if you use it to claim a product will sell. An argument may be faulted in many ways. It may involve many fallacies or none at all -it may just not fit the facts.

Fallacies can be fun, especially if you use the Latin names to hit people with. But don't be too obnoxious -and you may be committing a few fallacies in doing so (snob appeal, *ad hominem*, or, if things get really rough, *ad baculum!*).

1) appeal to force (ad baculum). Obviously war settles quarrels. But it doesn't settle intellectual arguments. Killing the other person doesn't prove he was wrong. Yet think of how often people assume something was 'settled a long time ago' just because of who won a war (or for that matter a vote or a ruling by a court). I am told the US Congress once decided to settle the value of *pi* by a vote.

2) appeal to the people (*ad populum*). Just because most people think a thing is true doesn't make it so. Once the majority thought the sun went around the earth.

3) snob appeal. This is the reverse of the above. Just because a 'rarefied' group holds a certain view about art or literature doesn't mean there's anything to it. Enlightened opinion once looked down on native herbal medicines.

4) you too (*tu quoque*). Parent: "Don't drink and drive" Kid: "You used to"–a standoff?, but not wisdom.

5) against the man (*ad hominem*). This is very common. A mathematician can be emotionally unstable, yet his math is true; a ruler who is a bad man might pursue wise policies. No matter how intensely we psychoanalyze the speaker, if we do not analyze the statement we haven't touched its truth. Attacking an opponent might be justified, if he is running for a position of public trust -his character is part of the reason to be for or against him.

6) appeal to authority (*ad verecundiam*). This is a fallacy in strict philosophy because we must use human reason. If one accepts any kind of revelation in theology, then this is the strongest kind of argument there.

Yet we cite experts and studies that we ourselves have not "checked out" or even fully understood. Often this is the best we can do. There isn't time to be up on everything. This is tolerable if it is necessary and if we keep in mind that experts can be wrong. It is most intolerable if the experts are pontificating in areas outside their expertise–Jefferson on the Bible or Einstein on politics.

7) begging the question (*petitio principii*). If you assume the conclusion as one of the premises, you really argue in a circle. Usually this is done without realizing it. Suppose we assume democ-

racy is the best form of government. Then faced with evidence that a regime tortures its people because of their race or religion, we still conclude it is the best government to be hoped for -since it is democratic. We have argued in a circle. This fallacy is not committed simply because a person already assumes the conclusion elsewhere. The conclusion must actually or implicitly be packed in among the premises used to argue for that very same conclusion. [Russell says Aquinas is not a first class philosopher because, as a religious man, he already knows where he wants to wind up. If that disqualifies an argument, no one could argue for any point, unless he had no idea where he was heading or he thought the conclusion he was arguing for was false! Bizarre!]

8) irrelevant conclusion (*ignoratio elenchi*). This involves drawing one conclusion when the premises or evidence leads to a different conclusion. It covers deductive mistakes and the abuse of statistics, etc. Evidence may show there is something wrong with our legal system, but the conclusion drawn is that foreign countries should comply with our rules.

9) red herring or pettifogging (raising a different issue to distract from the one at hand). This is more common in emotional harangues or in political obfuscation than in looking for the truth.

10) arguing from lack of evidence (*ad ignorantiam*). This does not appeal to the ignorance of the listener. It appeals to our common ignorance in the sense of lack of evidence. The argument is not always fallacious -it depends on whether we are in a good position to have the information that does not show up. To say the moon has no kangaroos because we have not found any, is now a pretty good argument. This is because if there were such, we should have found evidence by now. To say that Rigel or Sigma Dorado have no planets, because we have not found any, is a poor claim. At present, we have little reason to think we could find them, if they were there.

11) complex question. Have you stopped beating your wife yet? The question cannot be answered straightforwardly because it is really 2 or 3 questions: Do you have a wife? Did you beat her? Have you stopped this behavior yet?

This strategy is a favorite of courtroom tricksters but shouldn't bother anyone who is sincere. One simply refuses to take the question as presented but takes it apart carefully.

12) misusing relative terms.

Germany is small(er than Russia).

Germany is large(r than Andorra).

Therefore, Germany is large and small.

If we think not merely in terms of words, but of what they are about, how often would we make this type of error?

13) hasty generalization. You take a few cases and jump to a conclusion. Particular cases don't add up to a universal rule (even if you have many) unless: a) you run through all possible cases [The square of an integer cannot end in 2, 3, 7 or 8. We know this without checking the infinite set of integers because it is possible to group the numbers into a few kinds and then check these.] or b) there is some natural or necessary connection between the individual instances and the general case (hydrochloric acid + sodium hydroxide—> sodium chloride + water. This is a general rule, though only tested in a few cases.). This is the problem of induction.

Yet although we can't be perfectly sure of most other types of generalizations, we can't function without them. We can't test every snowflake for its temperature.

Then when is a generalization hasty? It depends on the type of subject matter involved. Generalizations in human affairs are especially shaky because of human variability and freedom. The more evidence, the firmer the ground.

14) false dilemma. Do you like Michelangelo or Leonardo? Do you like the Yankees or the Mets? There are other choices or both or neither. It may be common to think in little sets of two, little dyads. But we should ask: Are we forced to choose between these two? Do they exhaust the whole?

15) black and white. This allows a choice of only two extremes in cases where there are intermediate shadings. There is something between broad daylight and dark night or between cold sober and dead drunk. Defining the end of twilight is fruitless but still there is twilight. This fallacy should be held together with the next one.

16) fallacy of the beard. This excludes extremes (in cases where there are extremes) because there are grays. Just because it is difficult to state how many drops of vodka make a man inebriated, doesn't justify denying this man is drunk.

17) composition. (claim what is true of the parts must be true of the whole). Every person will die, therefore the human race will die. The flip of this is:

18) division. (claim that what is true of the whole is true of the part). A Ferrari is expensive therefore its seat belt is expensive. A boar is large therefore its eye is big.

19) amphiboly. (sentences with two meanings "The shooting of the hunters was horrible"), equivocation, puns. It is necessary to reason with analogies, different depths of meaning, irony, anagogical (spiritual or mystical) senses, etc. But they do not fit any formal system of logic and you must be alert to what you are doing.

20) *ignotum per ignotius* (explaining) the unknown or obscure by the more unknown or obscure. A theory may be very complex or difficult to understand. The four color theorem had to be proven by computers. That doesn't make it wrong.

But what worth is an explanation that is even more opaque than the original query. To explain time (obscure) by chronons or atoms of time (more obscure) may be an example of this. We can hardly say we have shed light on something, if we have only embedded it in a deeper darkness.

Footnotes

1. The collection of Aristotle's logical treatises is the *Organon*. *The Basic Works of Aristotle*, ed. Richard McKeon, Random House, New York 1970.

2. For Frege, et al., see our reading list.

3. For the Russell contradiction and the theory of types: see *The Principles of Mathematics*, Cambridge, 1903, pp.101- 107 and 523-528 respectively. [Second edition, W.W. Norton, New York] For Russell-Frege, see Frege, Gottlob, *Philosophical and Mathematical Correspondence,* (tr. Hans Kaal, University of Chicago Press, 1980), pp.130-133.

4. Hume, David, *A Treatise of Human Nature*, (edited by Ernest C. Mossner), Penguin Books, Baltimore, 1969. See pages 114-115, 299-311, for example.

5. Marx, Karl, *The Communist Manifesto*, (tr. Samuel Moore), Regnery, Chicago, 1954.

6. Popper, Karl, *The Logic of Scientific Discovery*, New York, 1959, p.278.

7. Ferdinand de Saussure's *Course in General Linguistic*s (tr. Wade Baskin), McGraw Hill, New York, 1966, might be a good launching pad for the philosophy of language. The quote about anthropology is from Thomas Prufer.

8. Duhem, Pierre, *The Aim and Structure of Physical Theory*, (tr. Philip P. Wiener), Atheneum, New York, 1962, pp. 183-190.

9. Frege, Gottlob, *"On Sense and Reference"* (tr. Max Black in Translations from the Philosophical Writings of Gottlob Frege, New York 1962).

10. Another tapestry of analogy from the *Republic* is the Divided Line. An allegory has multiple correlatives. A parable has one main point. Though some (e.g., the *Prodigal Son*) have many.

Metaphysical Tools

Causes

Outline
Aristotle's four causes with examples
More complex examples
Do all things have all four causes?
Are there other kinds of causes?
Clarifications about causes

Why did Rome fall? Why does an apple fall? How is silk formed? What is a rainbow? Who painted the Lascaux caves? How is beer made? Paper? Stain glass? What is a caterpillar just before it becomes butterfly? Why are giraffes' necks so long? Why do some people have green eyes?

We wonder about causes. But what is a cause, what does cause mean? Are there different kinds of causes?

Why does the Leaning Tower of Pisa lean? Was it a bad design, a bad architect, defective materials, soft earth, or could it have been done deliberately? More than one of these could be the answer. There are many types of cause.

Aristotle developed a theory of four 'responsibles' or causes[1] They are now commonly called the 1) material 2) formal 3) efficient and 4) final causes.

Take Michelangelo's *Pieta* as an example.

The material cause is the 'that from which' a thing is made. The marble.

The formal cause is the shape, form, paradigm, structure imposed on the matter. In a richer sense it is the essence, the 'what it is' or the 'what it is/was to be something'. Here it is Mary holding the newly-dead Jesus.

The efficient cause is the maker of a thing, the agent that does a deed, the reality that pours being. Michelangelo. The final cause is the goal, purpose, reason. Here, to decorate St. Peter's. There could be more than one purpose -to make money, to become famous, to glorify God.

Not everything we can say about a thing is a cause. For example, when the statue was made (1498-1500) is not a cause. Let us look at the four causes in more detail.

Material: An axe doesn't rust because it is an axe, but because it is of iron. The properties of the material, not what it was worked into or by whom, explain the rusting.

Formal: Wood can be made into a chair or a door. And a chair could be made of wood or metal. So what a chair is, is mainly its form not its material. Material properties are involved–if wood were sticky it wouldn't do for a chair.

[What-it-is-to-be a thing shows different faces, particularly in beings that can experience themselves. What it is to itself and what it is for something else. What it was to be Alexander was one thing for Alexander and quite another for those that fought him. Also, Alexander may have had very little self-understanding so we must distinguish what a thing truly is and what it is to itself. <Is this related to George Berkeley's claim that to be is to be perceived (esse est percipi) and that a thing truly exists in being perceived by God?>

A thing may be more real to an attentive mind than it is even to itself. A stop sign says stop to me but it doesn't seem to mean much to itself. This can get deep and mysterious quickly. What-it-is-to-be-a-tree is a fairly definite thing to me, but what is it to the tree?]

Efficient and Final: Distinguish carefully. The efficient cause of a car and of its motion are different. Workers made the car, the driver and the internal combustion of gasoline move it.

The purpose of a bridge is to cross a river, but the purpose of the bridge builder may simply be to make money.

The form of a car is both a design of the engineer and its incarnation in a car. The former can exist without the latter, e.g., Leonardo's inventions and the latter without the former, e.g., if a thing is made accidentally.

Before going further we must confront a challenge made by David Hume -that we cannot know causes at all. [2]

Billiard ball X hits billiard ball Y and knocks it in the hole. Hume would claim what we really perceive is a series: X moves; X and Y touch; X stops and Y moves; Y falls in the hole. We see one event happen and then another event happen. We never perceive causal connections. We associate these two events. If one always follows the other, we claim the first causes the second. This is unjustifiable because a constant conjunction is not a real causal connection. Many subsequent philosophers buy Hume's rejection of (efficient) causality. Their task is to explain the physical world and moral responsibility in acausal terms.

Those who reject Hume, instead of causality, might argue as follows: It is true that we do not perceive efficient causes in the sense of perceiving inner connections (since they are inner). But we intuit or understand connections -some necessary, others incidental -between things. In thinking, we go beyond perception. Further, not every constant conjunction conjures causality, at least not to humans. The rooster's crow doesn't make the sun come up, although he may think so. Humean thinking doesn't fit human thinking.

Even supporters of Hume may distinguish among different kinds of association–so we return to the kinds of causes.

i) Who killed John Kennedy? We are looking for the efficient cause. Detectives also look for the motive. *Cui bono* (to whose good) was the crime. This principle links final to efficient cause. Guessing the purpose may help us find 'who done it'. But finding out who, may not tell us why.

ii) In artifacts, like clothes and tools, form is closely linked to purpose. Shoes have leather as matter, shape as form, cobbler as maker, protection or adornment as purpose. 'Form follows function' -a vase and a violin are formed for what they are for.

iii) Material cause has the wider sense of 'that from which' or that which gets formed. The words of a poem are its matter, their combination its form, 'poet' means 'maker', the goal might be to charm or curse. Similarly, a collection of facts could be the matter and a theory about them a form.

iv) Physical structures are form-matter complexes or matter as formed in a certain way. Ethyl alcohol and dimethyl ether have the same matter but different forms–likewise, cyclohexane and hexene. But carbon itself is a form made up of 6 protons, 6 neutrons, 6 electrons. The matter (here carbon) for one thing can be the form of a 'lower' or more elementary thing. Wood is the matter of the house but the form of xylem and phloem.

The modern search for the most elementary particles seems either a search for forms that have no other sub-forms as constituents or for a matter that has no form at all. The latter, Aristotle calls prime matter. For him there is always some structure in any real thing. So prime matter, though a real ingredient, cannot be isolated. Alien as all this may sound to modern scientific discourse, Werner Heisenberg connects indeterminacy at the quantum level with the structurelessness of prime matter. [3]

Causes can be grouped: matter and form are intrinsic to a thing; agent and purpose are outside or extrinsic to it.

Does each thing have all four causes?

A) Mathematicals (objects like circles, isosceles triangles, prime numbers, nth roots) are forms without matter. Even if the study of circles began with rolling logs, circles can be analyzed without worrying whether they are redwood or oak. Topology is an example of higher pure form analysis. It can be applied to pancakes and doughnuts but the theorems are often hopelessly beyond picturing. Because math leaves matter aside, you can be a good mathematician but a poor carpenter -but not exactly vice versa.

B) Nature or Natural Objects: Can a volcano anticipate or remember? Are there final causes within nature? Is nature directed from the outside? If providence guides us, then presumably it guides all natural things as well. [Although not everyone agrees even here. Moses Maimonides, in the *Guide for the Perplexed*, opposes those who hold that God takes care of e.g., individual ants. For him providence extends to man and, at most, to species of animals. [4] If you find partial providence perplexing, more common views are: 1) God supplies a purpose to every created reality. 2) God makes the world but is indifferent to its course -Deism. 3) There is neither creation nor Providence.]

In any case, unless a volcano has a mind, it has no purpose to itself and is without final cause in this sense.

What about purpose in biology? For Aristotle, things 'fit in nicely' -so nature must be purposeful. Teeth, for instance. Incisors in the front, just where we would want them. Molars in the back where there's room for grinding. It's too much to ask us to believe that it just all fell out that way. For Darwin, things also 'fit in nicely' and so seem to have a purpose. But they only fit because any that do not fit are eliminated -natural selection. Organisms are without purpose or 'teleology'. Jacques Monod says 'function follows form'. An organism occurs by chance, but what it does follows by necessity from what it is. [5]

A third view leaves room for purpose, not within nature, but in an understanding or directing mind without.

C) Science: What about purpose in physics or chemistry? Modern science no longer says the planets go in circular orbits because that is the perfect shape or because they seek something. They explain in terms of material properties (matter), arrangements like stereochemistry (form) or actions and forces (efficient causes). They avoid final causes, but don't necessarily deny them. And science has expressions that refer to goals, e.g., centripetal=center seeking.

Modern physics is full of talk of forces and formulas but silent about forms. Yet the word 'formula' means 'little form'. To some, formulas are simply functions or acausal parallels between sets. When I say a Sumo wrestler weighs four times as much as my son, I don't imply any causal nexus between the two. I simply announce a mathematical relation.

Newton said he did not know the cause of gravity and he would not frame one (*"Hypotheses non fingo"*). Whatever the cause of gravity may be, the same relation holds for the moon in its orbit and the apple in its fall. Yet Newton did think of science as a search for causes. Gravity as a cause and the cause of gravity are not the same. The first is a cause and the second is the cause of the cause.

To say either "mass warps the space around it" or "one mass attracts another at a distance" sounds like an efficient or material cause, i.e. agency or property of/in things.

The attempt to exorcise causes from science leads to some peculiar justifications of it. Such as the claim that science only rejects the false. Will the prince find Cinderella simply by rejecting an endless parade of suitors?

D) What about, not causes in nature, but causes of nature or the cosmos, as a whole? Elsewhere we consider philosophical arguments about God. Here we discuss a few views on origins -whether purely philosophical or not.

1) Animism peoples the woods and waters with indwelling presences that affect and/or are affected by what happens. What type of causes are involved? Essences? Makers? No causes? Is *Eos(Aurora)*, the rosy-fingered Dawn itself? Or the maker or keeper (or mascot or totem) of the dawn?

2)In the creation epic of ancient Babylon, *Enuma elish*, Tiamat(water) and Apsu(abyss) are uncreated principles. The cosmos (or the ordered cosmos) arises out of a primordial combat. Marduk defeats his (great great grand)mother Tiamat and then arranges the world out of her body. The world is ordered rather than created. The uncreated (or God) seems to be primordial stuff, the material cause of all. [6]

If this view sounds hopelessly primitive, parallels have been suggested with as un-primitive an opus as Hegel's *Phenomenology of Spirit*. Quentin Lauer says Hegel's notion of creation is 'God spreading Himself out to get to know Himself better'. [7] Hegel ends the work by speaking of Absolute Spirit 'foaming forth His own Infinitude' (*schäumt ihn seine Unendlichkeit*). If this is Hegel's notion, then in both cases the 'out of which' is the Self-Rearranging-All, whether conceived as Stuff or Spirit.

3) A watchmaker makes a watch and winds it up. He sells it and pays it no further mind. Deists hold that God supplies the universe with its matter, energy and existence, but then leaves it alone. God is the efficient but not the final cause. Nature's 'own way' is what science tackles. Likewise, each man goes his own way, pursues his own happiness. This view may satisfy the first cause argument, but it leaves an odd mystery: Would a rational God make a world that He didn't care about?

4) Aristotle's Deity seems to be the flip side of Deism. God is the final but not the efficient cause. The world is uncreated but there is a complete actuality outside the changing world. The universe seeks completion through eternal cyclical change. As a planet orbits the sun it "seeks the center" (centripetal acceleration), but it doesn't get there. Yet without the "motive", there is no motion. His idea of God is not easy to be clear on -nor was he a heliocentrist. But I think this metaphor an apt one.

5) In Genesis, God makes the world out of nothing. There is no previously-existing, other-than-God, stuff hanging around. God is the efficient, not material cause.

6) In Christian theology as expounded by Aquinas and others, God is cause in these senses:

i) Formal cause. God is not the internal essence but the external blueprint. Outside creation, God is the only "show in town", so what else would creatures be like, if not God. Each entity is a way in which an aspect of God can be manifested or participated.

ii) Efficient cause of being. As the one and only self-existing being, God gives to be all else.

iii) Efficient cause of remaining in being. God does not make a thing so solid that it could continue to exist even if God were not. To do so would be to give not just existence, but self-existence, to a thing. God is the preserver of all.

iv) Final cause. This last is tricky. God has no external goal to attain for Himself in creating. If He did, He would be lacking. The universe is not a final cause for God. But God is the final cause for creatures. To the extent that any being seeks its reality, it seeks the Pure Reality.

Are there other kinds of causes?

Three others are mentioned: a) exemplary, b) instrumental and c) deficient.

a) Exemplary causes are models. Your hero is Joan of Arc. You model your actions on hers. You certainly are affected by her, so she is a cause for you. None of Aristotle's four fit exactly. We call her an exemplary cause.

b) Instrumental causes are like tools. The brush is neither paint, nor painting, nor painter, nor purpose. I need my nerves and muscles to run, yet by themselves they don't normally take off. If I am the efficient cause, they are instrumental. Russian even has an instrumental case.

Averroës views all human efficient causality as merely instrumental. We are but brushes in the hand of God. To Aquinas, although God is the primary cause, human free action is a secondary but true efficient cause.

c) The cold of the poles is 'caused by' a lack of sunshine. Cold is explained by an absence of heat rather than any positive property, essence or action. So is darkness. Deficient causes are lacks.

To compare these 'extra' causes to Aristotle's four:

a) You copy Leonardo's Last Supper. You try to make your painting's form (internal to it) like the form of the model (external to it). So exemplary causes are like outside forms. God as formal cause is like an exemplary cause.

b) If someone painted with his fingers, he wouldn't be as precise as with a brush. But the fingers are counted with the efficient cause, the painter. So instrumental causes are extensions of efficient causes.

c) Oxygen is needed to stay alive, a lack of it causes death. Deficient cause might be viewed as a lack of efficient cause. On this idea, deficient cause is a new cause only verbally, i.e., only if we ask the wrong questions -ask the cause of cold rather than of heat.

Yet reducing these to Aristotle's four loses something.

Exemplary causes act in a unique way -they can do nothing at all. Babe Ruth inspires many a little leaguer. Even things that never existed or are badly understood can serve. A real life coward could be an exemplary cause of bravery.

The notion of instrumentality helps us distinguish between true causes and mere supporting cast. Did confusing how we know with what we know lead philosophy into a cul-de-sac? How do we get out of our own minds? We don't have to worry unless we are lost inside. We are not lost or locked inside if ideas are instruments for knowing reality. We are Locke'd inside if all we can know are our own ideas. [8]

Deficient causality points up an asymmetry in things. It is not obvious to a shivering man that "cold does not exist". Physics is correct to talk only of heat, radiant energy, molecular motion, etc. as true causes. But this isn't obvious -it has to be shown. One might have supposed two poles (hot/cold), (light/dark) etc. as actual forces. In fact, this sort of thing has been thought.

What is the nature of evil: Are there two poles -good and evil? Are these caused or personified by two opposite powers? Is this the solution of the Persian religious leader Mani? It is a common notion today. Or can these be explained by one reality and its lack? This is the solution worked on by Augustine. Pain, disorder, separation and even sin are ultimately negations, absences. Their causes are deficient, like the causes of dark and cold.

The concept of deficient cause can help avoid mistakes. 'Natural selection' is given as the origin of species but by itself it is a specious origin. Natural selection is a cause of death, of non-presence, of extinction. It tells why there are no brown bears on Baffin Island. But natural selection can't put a white bear on Baffin Island. As a deficient cause, it cannot account for the presence of anything. Earlier scientists looked for a positive cause of cancer like the cause of bubonic plague. Now some look to deficient causes (e.g., a defect on gene p53).

Clarifications about causes
   1) Is a cause prior to its effect?
   2) Does a cause lose what it causes?
   3) What are some common confusions about causes?

   1) People think of causes as prior to effects. But in the act of causing they seem to be simultaneous. A 'kid coloring a book' and the 'book being colored by the kid' are simultaneous. If the action takes time to be transmitted, the act of causing is either simultaneous or differs by just that time. The 'sun warming the earth' is either simultaneous with the 'earth being warmed' or eight minutes earlier depending on point of view (earth's or sun's).
   Certainly no cause can follow its effect. Knowing dates in history clears up many a fable or false explanation, e.g., if someone thought Communism was a reaction to Fascism.
   2) If a cause 'pours out being', does it lose what it pours? A pouring out of oneself, in the sense of material cause, seems to involve this. In the Babylonian creation epic, Tiamat is parcelled out. But an efficient cause does not lose in causing. A seamstress makes a dress. She does not lose the dress or herself in the process (though it takes some of her time, thread, attention, and skill). It takes her skill but it does not take her skill away. She may sell the dress, but then she loses it by selling it, not by making it.
   3) Let us look at four common confusions about causes.
   a) We distinguish between what is a cause and what isn't. An *occasion* provides a setting for an action. Henry II had Thomas à Becket murdered while he was saying Mass. The Mass was an occasion for the murder, not a cause. A *principal* is a very general

word for any basis or foundation whatever including causes, occasions, reasons, etc. A *reason* is usually a final cause (why did you do it?), but it has other meanings also (why don't you like her?).

b) To say that A causes B when, in fact, both have a third cause in common is to commit the common cause fallacy. I notice that when it's foggy on autumn mornings (A), it's hot in the afternoons (B). I think A causes B. But A and B are both caused by a common change in atmospheric conditions.

c) To presume that just because X is followed by Y, X must have caused Y, is to commit the fallacy of *post hoc ergo propter hoc* (after this therefore because of this).

d) To confuse the genesis or origin of a thing with its essence or what it is, is a fallacy. An atheist could build a very 'spiritual' church. A test tube baby is fully human even if its origin is not fully 'human'. Wisdom comes from the mouths of babes.

Though some thinkers constrict causes to only the efficient or even eschew them altogether, we find it very true and helpful to keep all types. They are high-thought tools that can do precise things.

Some Special Notions

Making/Doing/Thinking

Making has a product; doing does not.

To make is to make something. In making a house there is a product -the house. The product is: 1) the end of (purpose), 2) the end of (in time), 3) superior to and 4) separate from the making. The making aims at the house and stops when the house is completed. The house-to-be commands how we go about making it. We don't make an igloo and a cathedral in the same way. The house is so separate from the activity of making it that it "begins its life" when the making ends.

Dancing, having fun with your friends, bearing up under trials, being kind -these are not makings, not for products.

Each making and doing has its own excellence. The "reasoned capacity" or excellence of making well in general is art. There are many kinds of art. Architecture is concerned with building, persiculture with peaches, sculpture with statues. No matter how much science it uses, medicine is an art because it has a practical aim, healing or curing.

Each doing has its own excellence or skill -skiing and singing, for instance. The excellence that governs our deeds in general is practical wisdom or phronesis. Phronesis can't show you how to ski, but it must govern the skier. Skiing when you are desparately needed elsewhere or caring more about winning than about your friend's life can't be excused. A person who is a good painter we call a good painter. A person who is ethically good we call good simply, a good person. A bad man can be a good skier or artist.

Confusing making and doing can be harmful. Picasso and Wagner are not bad artists because they may have been bad men. Their works must be judged separately from their deeds. A movie might be well made and even true. Yet showing it in a certain situation may be sure to set off a riot. To show it because it is good art confuses aesthetics with ethics. Those who lose sight of doing view life as production not action. They may think our lives are meaningless unless we leave some achievement behind. This idea slides easily toward the notion that some of us are useless "unpersons". Thinking is an actuality (though at times thoughts seem just to hit us, to happen to us) but not all thinking is involved with doing, or making, with what is to be chosen, done or made. Mathematics has practical applications, but its theorems are not about things to be done. One reasons about a cube or prime numbers without deliberating about human action. Theoretical wisdom or sophia is its excellence.

Because there is a realm outside both making and doing, science and speculative philosophy are not subordinate to technology. This realm goes beyond morality, though not against it. [Friends go beyond courtesy but are not ungracious.] An upright life, a clear conscience, a peaceful and just political order, a plentiful land, an industrious city -these are great goods. But are they the highest goods? Or are they, like health, goods that set up the space for other things–enjoyment of friends, contemplation, play, etc.

So we have three sets of triplets: maker, making, made; doer, doing, deed; thinker, thinking, thought. The first three are very separate. The next three are less so. [What a person does forges/expresses his character.] Are the last three not separate at all?

Work/Play

Play differs from work in: 1) its goal and 2) its manner.
1) If you play tennis for the fun of it, you play. If you lift weights to build your build, you work out. Work is for something and is subordinate to that something. It's useful. [Is this why it is torture to be made to do useless work - digging a hole only to fill it in!?]

Play is for itself even if some other result occurs also. Walking to take in the scenery is not work. If this helps your heart that is incidental. You don't stop because your heart has improved. But if you walk as a messenger boy, you work.

Play displays itself in its manner also. It is playful. There's a give and take in it (like the play in a wheel?). Sports contests can be awfully earnest, but if they are submerged in earnestness, are they still play? No matter how intense, a contest is taken out of the stream of daily drudgery. [9]

The distinction between work and play relates to that between making and doing, but it is not quite the same. Work and play are distinguished by why a thing is done (for another, for itself). Making and doing are distinguished by what results (an external product or not).

Making can be fun. Thomas McGlynn enjoyed making statues. Though there is a product, the making is 'play'. In other cases, there is a product, but the activity is not fully subordinated to it. Kids play at making sand castles. But if you presented them with finished sand castles it wouldn't be any good.

Of course, some people's work may be play to them. Willie Mays was happy to be paid for doing what he wanted to do anyway, play ball. Perhaps here we should not call this work at all -and say instead that some people are fortunate that they can make a living at something truly playful.

There has been tectonic shift in the attitude toward work and play between the "ancients" and "moderns". Aristotle, while clearing the ground for what is to be the top science, says: "As more arts were discovered, and some were for the necessities of life, others for amusement, the inventors of the latter were naturally always regarded as wiser than the inventors of the former, because their knowledge was not for the useful." [*Metaphysics,* 981b16-19]

To "moderns" this sounds dead wrong. Who would honor Zworykin [10] or Naismith more than Pasteur or Stihl? Moderns value play, but as recreation–something that recharges us for work. Extended to thinking, the modern preference for the useful runs to thought that has practical applications and to a disparagement of any other kind of thought as idle dreaming, or even socially harmful. [Not all moderns are "moderns". Contemplative monasteries are a dramatic counterexample. But these have been suppressed in some countries where doctrinaire moderns came to power. Do they hate the very idea of thought or activity outside the scope of work, commodity, exchange, etc.? Why?]

Why this shift? Have huge advances in science and technology changed our attitude? Did the ancients undervalue experiment and technological advances because they had a different notion of nature? Did they downgrade work because they had slaves? Do moderns downgrade pure thinking on the belief that it cannot reach true reality? Or perhaps moderns have lost theological hope (as compared to the medievals).*

Yet regardless of which age thinks what, in itself play is superior to work in both its manner and its end. A playful give and take is obviously more fun than somber or humorless earnestness. What is done for itself is freer and more sovereign than what serves some other purpose.

This reversal may come from philosophical mistakes: 1) A confusion of making and doing looks for a product in all life's activities. 2) The false assumption that all goods are diminished when shared, makes even intellection competitive.

Is there an even more general tendency to lose the pliability and pliancy of play. Could this distortion be deeply rooted in a rejection of freedom and a preference for servitude? Is this part of the dark side of our nature? The Colisseum games are a horrible example. Do such things tell us that something very fundamental is awry?

Risking overkill, three more examples of the decline of play and free activity: 1) leisure 2) sports and 3) school.

1) Some ancients thought philosophy and other higher things were for the few -because they required leisure. [Was it the snobbery of a slave society?] However, they were right about needing leisure. But today there has come about a revolution the ancients

couldn't have imagined. The average American has 99 servants. [This figure is arrived at very simply -the energy consumption per person is divided by the caloric intake needed for one person. The figure is about 100. That's one for you and 99 for your electric lights, plumbing, car, heating, etc.] But instead of providing the leisure to make "everyone a (philosopher) king", leisure is decreasing. In contemporary America, the cycle of production-consumption has about reached the point where the 168 hours of the week are entirely blocked in.

2) While sports at school are supposed to be a playful sideshow to learning, they displace play and learning.

3) Learning itself is degraded into grades, credits. The word school comes from the Greek skhole, leisure. Student is from the Latin studere, to be eager. But today "to school" means to drill, to discipline.

If one divides verbs into those of work and those of play, where do "to live" and "to be" fit in? The "to be" is not subservient to something else -existence itself is play. Creation itself is *lila* (Sanskrit, play).

*A deep (historical and metaphysical) answer is that the "moderns" mix two immiscibles: Christianity remembered and Christianity rejected. They chuck out the creator God but keep ideas that make sense only if God truly is.

From Christian theology, they keep the ideas of absolute mastery, the primacy of efficient causality and the notion that the world can be exhaustively known yet could be radically other than it is. Rejecting God, let man float up into God's place. Now man wills to make the world in his own image. This is a heavy job. So we must work really hard.

[Many shifts: Infinite perfectibility replaces infinite actuality. Unending improvements replace endless goodness. Thinking is subordinate to willing–so science must serve technology. Despite talk about free thinking, understanding realities as they are in themselves is actually abandoned. Commodity and commotion crowd community and contemplation.]

"Modernity" is hard to "cure" since it is neither natural nor supernatural. The modern is not a pagan who takes things as he finds them, nor is he one for whom hope in radical transformation is anchored in God.

Post-modernity is forced upon us by the impossibility (and ugliness?) of the task. But modern man has forgotten how he got here. Post-modern thinking must go back to these premises, realize their incompatibility and rethink them. [11]

Post-modernity (post-modern conditions) without post-modern thinking is empty and dangerous. Frustration accelerates as we require of man a task both hideous and Sisyphean -that by his technology he turn himself into God -who doesn't need technology.

Immanent/Transitive/Transcendental

Immanent means remaining within, dwelling within. Transitive means passing from the subject to the object (in grammar). And more generally, passing out from or leaving the subject. "To hit" is transitive in grammar, "to go" is not. But the action of going, itself goes out from an agent, though it is not received by anyone. In that sense it is transitive rather than immanent. Thinking, loving, choosing, and being happy are immanent. Our feelings are immanent, the expression we give to them is not. If one person shows his feelings more, it doesn't mean he has stronger feelings. Some people seem to ignore the immanent, though it is hard to imagine how. Imagining is immanent.

Transcendent means above and beyond, running through all cases, not limited by categories, etc. Beauty, truth and the like are called transcendentals because all sorts of things can be beautiful, true, etc.

Theologians say God is both immanent and transcendent. He dwells within the creature, but is not conditioned or captured by the creature.

Simple/Composite; Parts/Wholes

To be simple is not to have parts. A composite has parts. A child's erector set has parts that can be taken apart. That's the easiest composite to think of. Some parts cannot be separated. We can't separate the color from the rose, the pitch of a note from its loudness, the shape from the marble, though we reduplicate the shape by making a mold.

Some are separated in thought, even if not in a physical object. Geometry thinks about separated shapes, even if they cannot actually exist separately.

In chemical compounds, elements lose their character. Sodium explodes in water, chlorine is a greenish gas. These qualities are lost when they join in table salt. Likewise for hydrogen and oxygen in water. One could say hydrogen is not hydrogen when it forms part of a water molecule, but it can be recovered when water is destroyed by electrolysis.

Parts can make a whole in different ways. Also, a whole can be a whole, or be one thing, in various ways. A heap of stones is one thing in a very diluted way. The parts are just juxtaposed. A living thing has a higher unity than a dead one. A tree has a higher unity than the same wood after it has been cut up and put in a heap.

What are the most fundamental parts: irreducible bits of matter or quanta of energy, atoms of experience, slices of consciousness, the act of existing?

What kind of thing counts as a unit, an individual, a whole? Is a Volvox an individual or a colony? Is a giant fungus an individual? Do we have to solve all this to think properly about individuals, substances, parts/wholes, the kinds of unity?

What kind of unity is a human being, the events of one's life, a community of people, the human race. What unity is the largest, highest and deepest of all?

Problem/Mystery

Gabriel Marcel contrasts a problem and a mystery. [12] A problem has borders to it. It has a horizon of expectations–what the answers could possibly be. "How can a town get pure water", "how can we balance the budget" -these are problems.

A mystery has depth. You can enter more deeply into it, but you cannot engulf it like an amoeba or surround it like a problem. "How should I live?", "what kind of a person are you?" -these are mysteries.

A problem is like a circle even if we aren't sure where the center or edge is. A mystery is like a deep funnel. Mysteries seem big and fuzzy, so the temptation is to turn them into problems. Totalitarian politics views people as problems. Some view philosophy as a project: -to overcome physical death, to prevent war or tyranny, to build a new society. These may be good things to strive for, but if thinking is subordinated to them–something is false, something is missing. It is a simple truth that we are mysteries to ourselves and to each other. How can we declare a clarity that is not there? If before thinking begins, we decide what its goal is, we may be cut off (*decidere*) from wonder and newness. If mystery is evicted, freedom and fun may slip away too.

Substance/Accident

We speak of a horse, a brown horse, a cloth, a soft cloth -but we don't speak of a brown or a soft. The brown has its existence in the horse. It does not have a free floating existence of its own. What exists in itself is substance. A quality, etc. that exists in something else we call an accident. The word may be unfortunate because it sounds like those qualities occur accidentally, just happen to be there –[from the Latin *accidere*–to happen].

Which takes us to an important question -which qualities or accidents are central to a thing? Does a horse have to be brown to be a horse? Must a zebra be striped, a giraffe have a long neck, a leaf be green. In some cases we answer without hesitation, in others we wonder. To perform photosynthesis, a leaf must be green, this quality is not just an add on.

Without solving the above query, we label three items related to substance: a) central points, essence b) non-essentials that always accompany a substance (inseparable accidents) c) non-essentials that do not always accompany a substance (separable accidents) A quaint example given for 'man' may illustrate each category: a=rational, b=risible and c=white.

If all humans happened to be white, being-white still would not be essential to being-human. The last category gives us little trouble. We know horses don't have to be brown, because we see non-brown horses. But what about the difference between the first two. Is risibility an essential ingredient of humanness? How would we find out?

Several other questions flood in: 1) Which things are substances -e.g., is part of a thing a substance? Is my arm a substance? The fruit of a plant or only the plant itself? A rock? Part of a rock? To solve these problems, do we need to sketch in a correct and true catalogue of (at least part of) reality and its kinds? To do logic (and even grammar) do we need a catalogue of what counts as a thing? 2) What is a general term or 'universal' like horse, mammal, animal? 3) If we use 'essence' for what a thing is, then: a) what are the essences of the various things around us and how do we find them? b) what is the relation between the essence and the individual being? c) what is the relation between the individual being and the group that has the same essence?

Or do things manifest themselves well enough that these questions are not to the point?

Controversial and difficult thinking is often on inseparable accidents. E.g., what are the differences between men and women? The essential differences are physical and reproductive. But are there other differences (in telling a story, in emotional make-up, in relating to space, etc.) which might ride along with the essential difference? Elements neither precisely essential nor so external that they just happen to be there as if pasted on from outside.

Do such differences exist? Philosophy can't solve this problem. It just contributes pointers.

Reductionism

We have all heard statements like: the moon is nothing but a big rock in space; love is nothing but instinctual urges; the brain is just a super-computer; the mind is nothing but the brain; history is just gossip; morality is simply a matter of convention.

Each of these involves the claim that something (x) is nothing but something else (y). If x is normally taken to be greater than y or more special than y, this is reductionism.

Poets used to complain that the scientific view of the heavens robbed them of its romance and magic. We could never sing about the moon the same way once we knew it as an airless and waterless rock about 240,000 miles away.

Scientists don't usually agree. They try to show connections from more complex phenomena to less. And they think of this as a big gain, not a loss.

Suppose, for example, anthropologists relate the customs and beliefs of a people to the way they make a living. This, in turn, is related to their geography and hence the biology of their animals or their agriculture. This is related to earth science and evolution. These are related to physics and chemistry, which are connected to mathematics (crystal structures in chemistry, for example). Finally, mathematics is related to logic.

Scientists think our understanding is greatly increased when such a chain can be sketched out. And there is beauty in seeing so many relations and connections. But it is one thing to relate customs to geography -it is another thing to reduce them to it.

Is reductionism a fallacy? There seem to be two problems here: one is logical, one is metaphysical.

1) If x and y exist and x truly contains more than y, we can let x=y+z. Then in saying x is nothing but y, we are really saying y=y+z. Thus z=0, which contradicts the above.

If you say "romantic love is nothing but animal instincts", you are either saying "animal instincts are nothing but animal instincts" (y=y) with which all agree, or you are saying there is no magic, charm, mystery, hesitation, hurt, etc. about romantic love (z=0), with which, hopefully, no one agrees.

2) Some reductionists would modify this to say "y is the cause of x" or "x can be derived from y alone" even though they grant something in x that goes beyond y.

Is this a fallacy? It depends on one's metaphysics. If you allow an effect to exceed its total cause, it is not. But for many thinkers it is an axiom that an effect can not exceed its total cause, because otherwise part of the effect, z, is both caused (as an effect of y) and uncaused (since it jumps into existence beyond the scope of its cause, y).

Per Se/Per Accidens

A thing can act 'as itself', *per se* or *kath auto*, or it can act in some other way. When a shoe is used to protect someone's feet in climbing sharp rocks or walking through mud it is acting as it was meant to act, as it was designed. It is acting as a shoe, as itself, according to what is essential to it.

A shoe can also be used to hold a door open or to keep a stack of papers from flying off the table. But then it is not being used as a shoe. It is merely something with sufficient weight to hold the papers down. It acts through qualities it shares with many things, a hammer, for instance. A shoe or hammer so used is acting 'according to something else' or *per accidens* or *kata symbebikos*.

Kata symbebikos behavior doesn't have to be false, phony, evil or inauthentic, but it is different. The difference lies in its relation to a thing's own nature or essence. You could say a thing puts less of itself into kata symbebikos action.

If the only thing anyone ever did with either hammer or shoe was to hold stacks of papers, why not replace both with something cheaper like a brick.

The distinction may grow in importance if we apply it to human reality. If all we do is eat and sleep, aren't we acting the way a shoe does when it merely holds the door open? If shoes only hold doors open, why the design -why the soft toe, high arch, strong heel. If humans just function as workers and consumers -why the songs and giggles, the tired voice, the pretty eyes. And deepestly why the wonder, love, sympathy, hope, or, for that matter, why the boredom?

Someone might counter: So what! -if the only use a shoe is put to is to hold a door open? Does it hurt the shoe or offend anyone? True, this hardly lets the potential of the shoe come in to play. But lots of potentials are frustrated. How many roe never make it into adulthood?

In any case, we can look at the design itself. A shoe is most a shoe, when it 'does its thing', when it is shoe-ing, when it gives bounce to runner and dancer, when it protects explorer from thorns and scorpions. A violin jumps to life in the hands of a master.

Before returning to the human, let us take an intermediate and difficult case -animals. If I raise chickens for meat and eggs in a barnyard, I can allow the chicken to 'do its thing', to cluck and peck a bit, to express its chickenness with a gallinaceous flair. If I raise them in tiny boxes and put contact lenses on them so they won't see well enough to peck at each other (an actual practice), their kath auto manifestation is suppressed almost completely.

Is there anything wrong with this? I find it hard to think about this kind of thing. Is it a moral question at all -a matter of what is good/evil? Is it an aesthetic question -a matter of what is beautiful/ ugly? Are the two related in some cases? [Can there be 'pretty' and 'unpretty' actions?]

To return to human behavior: If the brightest person in the world uses his intellect solely for looking for patterns in telephone books, isn't there something missing? To be fully human, is it enough not to hurt anybody and to contribute our share to the work pool? Perhaps morality and psychology can use this philosophical distinction. What is the kath auto action of humans? If we call such 'humaning', then what is real humaning? And exactly what importance does it have? How is it related to goodness and happiness?

One Thread of Metaphysics

It is hubris to raise, let alone claim to solve, the problem of the one and the many here. But it is a taste of more "advanced philosophy" as well as an example of how philosophers borrow from each other and talk directly to each other down through the ages. Also the problem (or mystery?) may underlie the theme that relates one to many -love. So we ask mercy and plunge in:

We begin with Parmenides.[13] He said Being is one. How could there be two beings? They would have to differ in some way. But they cannot differ in being–since that is how they are the same (both exist). Nor can they differ in non-being, since non-being is not. So there is but one Being, unchanging and neither generated nor mortal. IT IS or IS says it all! Since this doesn't seem to fit the facts, many have wrestled with this one. How can we explain a plurality of beings without granting non-being some sort of reality? Theories and interpretations thereof abound. Some say it is just a confusion of different senses of is or being.

[The rest of the version here is that of Aquinas.[14]] His theory goes something like this: Existence is not simply the fact that something is, but the act whereby it is.

He draws on Plato's Theory of Forms and Aristotle's notion of potency and act. For Plato, a reality such as Beauty has an existence above and beyond its individual instances. The individual instances 'participate' the form, but they do not comprise it or exhaust it. Beauty, e.g., is not just the sum of individual beautiful things nor an abstraction from what they have in common. Rather things are beautiful because they participate in the sovereign form Beauty Itself.

Aristotle explains physical change (and many other things) in terms of potential as a limiting, receptive factor and act as an active, real-making factor.

For Aquinas, what-a-thing-is (essence) is the limiting factor. It is real only with its to-be or act of existence. Beings are made up of these two components -essence and existence. There can be many beings if they receive their existence from a source. The source of existence cannot itself receive existence. Without any receptive or limiting factor, it is Subsistent Existence, Pure Act.

Limited beings participate Subsistent Existence somewhat like a Platonic form. They take part without taking apart. God is not parcelled out among creatures. What a creature is, is a partial likeness of God. That a creature is, is a free gift of God.

It is very difficult to speak of this theory because we tend to make the to-be into a thing (reification)–which cancels the theory.

Footnotes

1. Aristotle, *Physics,* Book 2, ch. 3-7
2. Hume, *Treatise of Human Nature*, p.223
3. Heisenberg, Werner, *Physics and Philosophy*, Harper and Brothers, New York, 1958, p.160
4. Maimonides, Moses [Moses ben Maimon], T*he Guide for the Perplexed,* (tr. M. Friedlander, Dover, New York, 1956), pp. 282-286.
5. For Aristotle's anticipation of evolutionary arguments, see *Physics* 198b18-33. For the opposite, see Darwin's *Origin of the Species* and Monod, Jacques, *Chance and Necessity*, (tr. Austryn Wainhouse, Vintage, New York, 1972).
6. The *Enuma elish* is translated by Alexander Heidel in *The Babylonian Genesis*, Univ. of Chicago Press, 1969 and by N.K. Sandars in *Poems of Heaven and Hell from Ancient Mesopotamia*, Penguin, 1989.

7. Quentin Lauer's expression I heard in a talk given by him. See also his *Hegel's Concept of God*, SUNY Press, Albany 1982.

8. Adler, Mortimer, *Ten Philosophical Mistakes*, Collier Macmillan, New York, 1985, p.14.

9. A many-faceted study of play is Johan Huizinga's *Homo Ludens: A Study of the Play Element in Culture*, Beacon Press, Boston, 1955.

10. Vladimir Zworykin was the main inventor of television. Apparently he lived to regret the use of his amazing invention. Some people blame the medium of television for the content shown. They might as well blame vowels and consonants for lies and obscenities. This is a confusion of causes. If the content of TV is an organized form of moral hideousness (a sort of modernized Colisseum), the blame is with the owners and producers, not the medium. The same electrons could bear truth and kindness.

11. Thomas Prufer, to whom I am indebted for so much, says, "Heidegger has taught us an interplay of hiddenness and manifestation which is beyond the dialectic or push-pull of inner and outer... of acceptance and rejection of inheritance and tradition: he has taught us that the otherness of hiddenness and truth to each other is not an otherness of loss or contradiction: they rest in each other; they are not violently wrested from each other. Perhaps Heidegger indicates a way both to a rediscovery of Greek philosophy and to a rediscovery of Christian theology, ..." *Recapitulations*, CUA Press, Washington, DC, 1993, p.69.

12. Marcel, Gabriel, *Creative Fidelity*, (tr. Robert Rosthal, Noonday Press, New York, 1964), p78-80. Marcel himself seems fuzzy -but maybe that helps him show fuzziness as fuzziness to those who think only in univocal terms.

13. For the fragments of Parmenides, et al. see Kathleen Freeman's *Ancilla to the Pre-Socratic Philosophers*, Harvard Univ. Press, 1966.

14. This precis of Aquinas' is indebted to Charles Hart's *Thomistic Metaphysics*, Prentice-Hall, Engelwood Cliffs, 1959.

Metaphysics

Reading List

"You know, Phaedrus, that's the strange thing about writing, which makes it truly analogous to painting. The painter's products stand before us as though they were alive, but if you question them, they maintain a most majestic silence. It is the same with written words; they seem to talk to you as though they were intelligent, but if you ask them anything about what they say, from a desire to be instructed, they go on telling you the same thing forever. ... And when it is ill-treated and unfairly abused it always needs its parent to come to its help, being unable to defend or help itself." [Plato, *Phaedrus* 275e, tr. R. Hackforth]

How can we get fossilized words into living thought? I can't think of any sure-fire way. Discussing books with others can help. With the information retrieval systems available today, the problem for most of us is not how to get hold of a work, but how to get some "hold", "purchase" on it.

So this list is not one of editions, dates and cities.Rather it tries to get over the first hurdle in reading the listed authors. Some philosophers are relatively approachable. One can walk into a bookstore and take on Locke or Nietzsche right away. Few will find Kant or Scotus so accessible.

In some cases secondary literature helps overcome the opacity. We recommend Frederick Copleston's *A History of Philosophy* for its gentle explanations, balanced discussions and further leads.

If a philosopher can be "appropriated" in a fairly direct way in the form you are apt to find him, we simply note chief work(s). We limit ourselves to 30 entries from Western philosophy -which means leaving out a lot: Croce, Bergson, Bonaventure, Schopenhauer, etc.

1. The pre-Socratics survive in fragments. A collection of these is Kathleen Freeman's *Ancilla to the Pre-Socratics*. Socrates himself appears in the works of Plato. How far his words there express Socrates' own ideas we leave to scholars.

2 . Plato speaks metaphorically and on many levels. One reason may be so that those of lesser understanding will profit on their own proper level rather than having their limited wisdom destroyed (because they grasp part of an argument) but not replaced (because

they do not grasp another part). Without overriding the sophisticated scholarly analysis of Plato, we do think he can be read fairly directly with profit. *Apology, Crito, Phaedo, Symposium, Republic*. Keep on going or come back. The Neo-Platonists are important on their own. Plotinus -*Enneads*, Porphyry -*Isagoge*, Proclus -*Elements of Theology*.

3. Aristotle's style may be difficult but once you get through a section you have the impression that he has said what he means. *Nicomachean Ethics* is a good place to start. *The Poetics*, the logical works, -keep going or get help.

4. Epicurus is available in his *Letters, Principal Doctrines* and *Vatican Sayings* and through Lucretius' poem *On The Nature of Things*. Epictetus -*Enchiridion*.

5. We do not present Jesus as a philosopher. But in as much as Christian ideas are items for philosophical reflection also -the sources are the New Testament and the mainstream historical development of Christianity.

6. Augustine -the *Confessions* is a good place to start. *On Free Choice of the Will* and *On the Immortality of the Soul* are essential to our discussions here.

7. Boethius -*The Consolations of Philosophy*.

8. The medieval theologians present a special problem. Their philosophical insights may be buried in a theological question few readers would even look at. John Scotus Eriugena -*On the Division of Nature*. He is also called John the Scot (although he was Irish, not a Scot -don't confuse with John Duns Scotus who was a Scot). Abelard is approachable through secondary sources.

9. Anselm -*Proslogion* and *Monologion*.

10. Averroës and Avicenna -major works are not available in translation. Secondary sources and what is translated is a big help. Moses Maimonides -*Guide for the Perplexed*.

11. If schools of philosophy were political parties, Aquinas would probably get more votes than anybody. Yet you can't walk into a store and come out with his philosophy in a single volume. The *Summa Theologica* is massive. The questions there contain pro and con arguments and a resolution. Aquinas himself distinguished philosophy (based on human reason) sharply from theology (the study of revelation). But the two occur together in his work. For a

reader not attuned to or interested in speculative theology this is a difficulty. However, since Thomists are so numerous, help is available.

12. Duns Scotus' works are hard to come by and hard to get through. We recommend starting with Allan Wolter's translations and other works. Ockham -*Philosophical Writings* (a selection translated by Philotheus Boehner).

13. Descartes -*Meditations and Discourse on Method* are readily available. The reader is warned: Descartes may be putting forth ideas and undermining them at the same time.

14. Spinoza -*Ethics*

15. Leibniz -*Monadology, Theodicy, Discourse on Metaphysics*

16. Hobbes -*Leviathan*

17. Locke -*An Essay Concerning Human Understanding, Two Treatises of Government*

18. Berkeley -*A Treatise Concerning the Principles of Human Knowledge*

19. Hume -*A Treatise of Human Nature, Enquiry Concerning Human Understanding*

20. Kant -Start with the *Foundations of the Metaphysics of Morals* and then gear up for the *Critique of Pure Reason.*

21. Hegel -*The Phenomenology of Mind* is a main work. Secondary literature is almost required. A problem is that it is usually heavily interpreted. For a time most Hegelians were Marxists which made the pure Hegel even harder to get at. Quentin Lauer and Kenneth Schmitz may be helpful.

22. Marx -*The Communist Manifesto* and *Capital*; Mill - *Utilitarianism and On Liberty.*

23. Darwin -*The Origin of the Species, The Descent of Man.* Most of the discussions here are not philosophy. We include him here because of the impact of evolutionary notions and because of the need for a philosophical biology. Teilhard de Chardin's *The Phenomenon of Man* is a philosophizing and theologizing on evolution.

24. Kierkegaard and Nietzsche -readily available. Both are not so much major philosophers as intense and personal Christian (Kierkegaard) and anti-Christian (Nietzsche) thinkers. Kierkegaard

is a special kin to Pascal -*Pensées* and *Provincial Letters*.

25. Husserl -*Cartesian Meditations, Experience and Judgment, Logical Investigations*. Definitely worth the struggle and what a struggle it is without help. But there is help. Robert Sokolowski explains and gives very clear examples in *Husserlian Meditations*. Gottlob Frege is a sort of founding father of contemporary (=post-Hegel) thought. Translations from the *Philosophical Writings of Gottlob Frege* are available (ed. Max Black and Peter Geach).

26. Heidegger -*Being and Time, An Introduction to Metaphysics*. Heidegger is usually taken to be talking about man when he is talking about being. Thomas Prufer is a keen interpreter -*Recapitulations*.

27. Anglo-American -Ludwig Wittgenstein is neither Anglo nor American but he shares with this "school" an emphasis on logic and language. *Tractatus Logico-Philosophicus* and the *Philosophical Investigations* are his chief works. *Classics of Analytic Philosophy* (ed. Robert R. Ammerman) contains classics of Russell, Strawson, Moore, Quine, Austin etc.

28. Recent Continental -In Europe, the interest is more on metaphysics or, at least, on existence and the puzzle of being human. Sartre, Camus, Marcel, Jaspers, Buber, Berdayev are available. Here is a place to mention some thinkers who might be grouped as/with theologians: Maurice Blondel, Vladimir Solovyov, Pavel Florensky, Karl Rahner. Bernard Lonergan (not a Continental) -*Insight*. Jacques Derrida (deconstructionism) and Michel Foucault (structuralism) have taken yet other paths.

29. Perhaps like wine, the thought of one's own time must age a bit before we can judge it. I find Joseph Pieper (born 1904) a man of fresh wisdom. *Happiness and Contemplation, On Love* and *Leisure: The Basis of Culture*.

30. Other: We do not list Oriental and other sources because we could not do them justice. However several are cited in the text. Again many novelists write with a view on human nature and in that sense have philosophical claims. But where to stop?